INTRODUCTION

As teachers and consultants, we have worked in elementary classrooms for years and have experienced the many challenges of teaching well. Recently we've been working with teachers and nine- to eleven-year-old students to improve teaching and learning in science. We've used nonfiction trade books extensively. In addition, we have taught students strategies for reading nonfiction with better comprehension. We are excited by the results—students are more interested and motivated, and they are learning more. We hope that after reading this book, you'll try some of our ideas and experience similar results. All of the lessons presented here have been field-tested in elementary classrooms in Holland, Michigan, USA. While we were writing this book, we were contacted by the science coordinator at Holland Public Schools, who informed us of the district's plan to move away from textbook-driven science instruction and incorporate a hands-on curriculum. There was also concern about students' informational reading skills. Teachers realized the importance of having students read nonfiction but felt the science textbooks they were using was too difficult; as a result, they found themselves supplementing the textbooks with trade books from the school library. The teachers thought the students enjoyed reading the trade books; however, trade books were in short supply. The science coordinator, like the teachers in Holland, felt the use of trade books was a valuable way to complement the hands-on aspect of the science curriculum as well as motivate students to read more informational text. If trade books were made an integral part of the revised curricu-

5

lum, then the district would most likely purchase class sets of various titles. The science coordinator was looking for assistance with this endeavor at the same time we were in the process of selecting sites to field-test our materials and lesson plans.

Holland Public Schools serve diverse students with a variety of needs. Of the total student population, 64.3% are Caucasian, 26.1% are Hispanic, 5.1% are Asian, 4% are African American, and fewer than 1% are Native American. For many students, English is not their first language. There is also a wide socioeconomic range within the ten elementary schools in the district. For instance, at Van Raalte, Jefferson, and Holland Heights, over half the student population qualifies for the free or reduced-price lunches available to economically disadvantaged children through a U.S. federal government program. In addition, these schools have a high population of physically and mentally challenged students. This is in contrast to Harrington Elementary, where the majority of students come from middle- and upper-class homes. Our feeling was that Holland Public School District represented a cross-section of American society today. If our ideas and materials worked in Holland, we felt comfortable they would work in most school settings. So in August 1995, we formed a partnership with Holland Public Schools and our field-testing began.

Eleven fourth and fifth grade teachers in four elementary schools (Harrington, Holland Heights, Jefferson, and Van Raalte) volunteered for our pilot program. We established a monthly meeting with the participating teachers, the science coordinator, and the district reading specialist. At our first meeting we asked the teachers why they chose to get involved. Most told us that they were eager to learn how to integrate science and literature in ways that would be exciting for their students while at the same time reinforcing students' reading skills. Other teachers said they wanted to update their knowledge of science concepts and improve their teaching skills. All of the teachers in the pilot were very positive, optimistic, and motivated; we felt fortunate to be able to work with professionals of this caliber.

We purchased classroom sets of trade books with grant money donated by the Binda Foundation of Battle Creek, Michigan. Because we were unable to purchase enough

Fusing Science with Literature

Strategies and Lessons for Classroom Success

CARYN M. KING

PEG SUDOL

Pippin Publishing

ACKNOWLEDGMENTS

We would like to acknowledge gratefully the support we received from the following people and institutions: Allan Ten Eyck, Michelle Smart, John Mierz, Loretta Konecki, Dorothy Armstrong, Don Pottorff, and the M.Ed. in Reading graduate students in the School of Education, Grand Valley State University, Grand Rapids, MI; Marty Coon, Lara Johnson, Rita Riembold, Nancy Rottschafer, Elizabeth DeJongh, Marcia Hildebrand, Brenda Martinez, Mary Theisen, Phyllis Baldwin, Julie Walters, Scott Hoover, Sue Boote, Jon Toppen, Ethel Barense, and Ruth Hofmeyer, Holland Public Schools, Holland, MI; Dee Etter, Robin Tapia, and Jody Cameto, Marana Unified School District, Tucson, AZ; and Elizabeth Binda, Guido Binda, and Vern Boss, Binda Foundation of Battle Creek, MI. Above all we would like to thank David Sudol for his expert guidance.

Designed by John Zehethofer
Typeset by JayTee Graphics Ltd.
Edited by Anne Fullerton
Printed and bound in Canada by Friesens

Canadian Cataloguing in Publication Data

King, Caryn
  Fusing science with literature : strategies and lessons for classroom success

(The Pippin teacher's library ; 33)
Includes bibliographical references.
ISBN 0-88751-096-5

1. Science — Study and teaching (Elementary). 2. Literature — Study and teaching (Elementary). 3. Content area reading. I. Sudol, Peg. II Title. III. Series

LB1585.K55 1998   372.3'5044   C98-930476-0

CONTENTS

copies of every title for every classroom, we set up a schedule to circulate books among the teachers at the four participating schools. Teachers were also given a booklet containing the lesson plans to be piloted and an evaluation form to complete after teaching each one. During our monthly meetings, we discussed how the teachers taught each lesson, what did and didn't work well, and ideas for improvement. Because the teachers were using different trade books, our monthly discussions gave those who had not yet used a particular title the advantage of learning what teaching techniques had been most effective. Thus, as the pilot progressed, each lesson plan became more and more refined as it incorporated the experiences of the various teachers and students.

In between our monthly meetings, we visited classrooms and observed the trade books and lesson plans in action. (Two teachers were uncomfortable with being observed, so we respected their wishes and did not visit their classrooms.) Great things were happening! For instance, when we sat in on the lesson involving Sandra Markle's *Earth Alive!*, students were making insightful comparisons between changes they'd seen in their own neighborhoods and changes occurring in the Earth's crust. (Holland is a city currently experiencing significant growth in industry and population.) Students compared and contrasted their observations by discussing them and then created graphic organizers incorporating their prior knowledge with new concepts learned from *Earth Alive!* This was a valuable learning experience because students were able to make personal connections to the science concepts being addressed in the text.

In another lesson on the Earth's crust, students were conducting simple experiments to simulate natural changes within the planet. Acting as scientists do, students formulated hypotheses, made and recorded observations, formulated new predictions and hypotheses, and used trade books to find support for the results of their experiments. We heard students use terms associated with experimentation, such as *variable*, *hypothesis*, *observation*, *discovery*, and *validate*. Moreover, when they validated their results with trade books, they gained other valuable skills such as using a table of contents, an index, and a glossary, as well as skimming and scanning text.

Several teachers chose to incorporate additional books and writing into the lessons. For instance, after reading *Our Solar System* by Ian Graham, some students read David Drew's *Postcards from the Planets* and created a postcard of facts about each planet. Students laminated their postcards and actually sent them to parents and friends. In doing so, they learned how to address a postcard and how to write succinctly. In a lesson involving *Antonio's Rain Forest* by Anna Lewington, students wrote letters to Antonio, the Brazilian boy who narrates the text. They described for Antonio the ecosystems they had observed around the eastern shore of Lake Michigan where Holland is located, and they compared and contrasted the plant and animal life of their home to that of Antonio's home in the rain forest.

In summary, the teachers in our pilot program used trade books to help their students question, apply, analyze, and synthesize information—all important aspects of scientific literacy. Students told us that they felt using the trade books helped them become better readers and scientists. Of the 119 students we interviewed, the majority were able to recall and elaborate on concepts associated with ecosystems, weather, space, and the Earth.

Despite the success stories we have just described, we realize that teaching science in the elementary grades is difficult. We as teachers often feel underprepared, materials and space in the classroom for experiments are hard to find, curricular pressures mean many concepts have to be covered (often to be tested later), and science textbooks are difficult for students to read. Unless you love science and are willing to spend extra time planning to make it stimulating for children, science class can be a matter of simply reading and discussing the textbook. As a result, students often are not enthusiastic about science. We believe nonfiction trade books offer a solution to these problems, and we hope that our suggestions for using such books will help you feel better prepared to make science interesting and exciting.

We've written this book primarily for in-service classroom science teachers of nine- to eleven-year-olds. Not only do we describe specific reading strategies that students can use when reading nonfiction, but we also list nonfiction trade books for teaching various science topics. You can use the reading strategies that we describe with many populations and in subjects other than science. For example, middle school and high school content area teachers could also use them.

The next chapter describes how we chose the nonfiction trade books featured in this book. We devised a checklist that acts as an easy-to-use guide for selecting quality nonfiction. We selected titles based on the following criteria: accuracy, organization and layout, cohesion of ideas, specialized vocabulary, and reader interest. Next we provide detailed descriptions of all the reading strategies that we use. We describe graphic organizers, K-W-H-L, a discussion web, a reading roadmap, an expectation outline, an anticipation guide, a knowledge rating, and the vocabulary self-collection strategy. These strategies promote active student involvement in the pre-, during, and postreading stages.

The remainder of the book highlights four specific topics common to science curricula developed within the past ten years. These topics are the Earth's crust, the environment and ecology, space, and weather. Each chapter highlights particular books and includes detailed lessons describing how to use selected reading strategies to teach students both the scientific objectives and how to read nonfiction. We also include an annotated bibliography of nonfiction trade books suitable for a wide range of student abilities. We hope that as you read these lessons you'll discover additional ways to use nonfiction trade books in your own science classroom.

SELECTING QUALITY

NONFICTION TRADE BOOKS

More and more teachers are using trade books to teach language arts and content area subjects. Although fiction has been the most popular genre, nonfiction titles are also widely available. There are lots of compelling reasons to use trade books in the classroom. First and perhaps most important, nonfiction trade books focus on a single topic, covering it in great detail and providing for depth of understanding. Textbooks, on the other hand, must cover much of an entire subject, and in doing so often omit or trivialize important aspects of individual topics. Using trade books also exposes students to a variety of genres. Because the students in our classrooms are diverse, it makes sense that the reading materials we use should also be diverse. Finally, today's nonfiction trade books are very aesthetically pleasing. They often contain beautiful, full-color photographs and interesting graphics that capture the attention of the reader. When students experience the pleasure of such literature, it is more likely they will want to continue to read. Thus, trade books can be one way to motivate reluctant readers.

One of the problems with using trade books in the classroom, however, is the selection of appropriate content-related titles. In her article "Thirteen Steps to Becoming a Children's Literature Expert," Patricia Richards points out that "almost overnight teachers have been asked to become children's literature experts, knowing the perfect book for every situation, every reader, every curriculum area." This chapter offers help with this problem by providing tips and guidelines for choosing nonfiction.

When we began to search for titles to include in this book, we reviewed *Books in Print, Book Review Digest,* and *Book Review Index,* checking under the following headings: the Earth's crust, the environment and ecology, space, and weather. We also consulted book distributors and found them to be very accommodating. Most in North America have toll-free telephone numbers and send free catalogs to interested teachers. In some instances, we used the distributors to order trade books that were piloted in this project. We continued our search by checking periodicals such as *School Library Journal, Booklist, Childhood Education,* and *Horn Book Guide.* Since we were looking for nonfiction trade books to use in science classrooms, we also consulted the periodicals *Science Books & Films* and *Science and Children.* All of these sources were in our university library. We found them easy to use since titles are listed by both subject and author. Of course, school or district media specialists can offer invaluable assistance in tracking down trade books and can often suggest references to consult for any number of topics or subject areas.

Once we located nonfiction trade books, we faced a more daunting problem: how to select good ones to use in this book. Consequently, we developed a checklist. We believe it will be especially useful for busy classroom teachers who need a quick and efficient method for reviewing and evaluating trade books, and who, like us, have limited funds.

We looked at a number of resources when designing our checklist. We used Richard and Jo Anne Vacca's adaptation of the Judith Irwin and Carol Davis Readability Checklist and the concept of considerate text that Bonnie Armbruster and Thomas Anderson describe in their book *Content Area Textbooks.* For additional ideas, we consulted Eileen Burke and Susan Glazer's *Using Nonfiction in the Classroom.*

The first section of our checklist considers *accuracy.* Often teachers don't take the time to think about a book's accuracy. We assume that if the information is on the page, it must be correct. Yet that's not always the case. To check for accuracy, we asked these questions: Is information on the author's experience and expertise provided? Are photo credits included? Are references cited throughout the text or included in a bibliography? And, of course, is the information current?

Checklist for Evaluating Nonfiction Trade Books

Topic: _____ Price: _____

Author: _____ Library Call No.: _____

Title: _____

Publisher: _____ Copyright Date: _____

Series: _____ ISBN: _____

Total Score: _____ Recommend? _____ For Whom? _____

3 = meets all or most criteria   2 = meets some criteria   1 = meets few criteria

Check all that apply, or write NA if not applicable. Then select an overall score for each category.

____ **Accuracy**
- information about author expertise/experience given
- photo credits given
- references cited throughout text or provided in bibliography
- information current and accurate

____ **Organization and Layout**
- note inclusion and quality of table of contents, chapter and section headings, summaries, index, glossary, charts, graphs, maps, illustrations
- predominant pattern of organization (cause/effect, compare/contrast, problem/solution, time order, description) appropriate

____ **Cohesion of Ideas**
- major ideas logically connected throughout
- sentence-level ideas logically connected to one another
- reader's probable background knowledge respected
- conceptual load appropriate
- irrelevant details avoided
- good model of expository writing provided

____ **Specialized Vocabulary**
- defined when introduced
- defined in pictures with captions or labels, or clarified visually
- defined in glossary

____ **Reader Interest**
- has aesthetic appeal
- has colorful illustrations or photos
- uses appropriate format
- has positive role models for gender and ethnicity
- has activities and/or experiments within the text that are motivating

Annotation:

From Sudol, Peg, & King, Caryn M. (1996, February). Teaching Reading: A Checklist for Choosing Nonfiction Trade Books. *The Reading Teacher*, 49(5), 422-424. Reprinted with permission of Peg Sudol and the International Reading Association. All rights reserved.

The second section involves *organization and layout*. This part examines if the text is arranged in a way that makes it easy to read and use. For example, is there a table of contents that gives an overview of the book? Do chapter and section headings provide information about the important concepts? Do an index and glossary aid the reader in finding specific information? Are visual aids such as charts, graphs, maps, and illustrations used to assist comprehension? Moreover, because well-written nonfiction should be organized to allow the reader to see relationships among concepts, this section also looks at the predominant pattern of organization and asks if it is the most appropriate for explaining the concepts.

The third section of our checklist is *cohesion of ideas*. Ideas should be unified and logically ordered from beginning to end. Both unity and coherence are vital within individual paragraphs as well as throughout the text. Unity within a paragraph occurs when the text includes words or phrases that signal connections explicitly (for example, *because, therefore, as a result*) so that the reader doesn't have to make too many inferential leaps. Unity of the whole occurs when all ideas belong together and develop a thesis statement. Another concern here is whether the text respects the reader's background knowledge. Does the author assume the reader has more prior knowledge than is likely? An appropriate conceptual load is important as well. Are abstract concepts introduced one at a time and accompanied by a sufficient number of concrete, relevant examples, or does the author include irrelevant details? In general, is the text a good model of expository writing?

The fourth section is *specialized vocabulary*. By necessity, nonfiction contains much technical vocabulary. Typically, nonfiction trade books define vocabulary in one of three ways: the text may define special words as they are introduced; pictures with captions or labels may define and clarify the vocabulary; or a glossary may give definitions for technical terms. In each of these cases, the vocabulary needs to be explained in a way the reader can understand, at a lower level of abstraction than the word being defined.

The fifth section of our checklist is *reader interest*. Quite simply, we want to know if the text grabs and holds the reader's attention. Is the text visually attractive? Does it include colorful illustrations or photos? Is the format (page and print size) appropriate? Are positive gender and racial/ethnic role models provided? Will the students be excited by the activities and experiments described? Will they want to read this book?

After completing the checklist for a particular title, we find it helpful to write a short annotation. Usually, we list the major concepts the book addresses. Then we note any unusual or outstanding features. The annotation is especially handy when reviewing many books on the same topic.

We used this checklist to evaluate the many science trade books that we reference in this book. The process didn't take very long, and when we finished filling out the checklist, we were able to decide quickly and easily whether the book was worthwhile for our purposes. We hope that you, too, will find this checklist helpful in selecting nonfiction trade books for teaching content area subjects.

. . . .

COMPREHENSION STRATEGIES FOR READING NONFICTION TRADE BOOKS

This chapter describes the strategies used in the lessons presented in the remainder of this book, including graphic organizers, K-W-H-L, the discussion web, reading roadmap, expectation outline, anticipation guide, knowledge rating, and vocabulary self-collection strategy. We chose these particular strategies because we believe they are effective means of teaching important scientific skills such as creating awareness, encouraging exploration, prompting inquiry, and applying scientific concepts to our world, while at the same time teaching processes that skilled readers use.

For instance, in a lesson described in the next chapter, a graphic organizer is used to create awareness of the many ways natural causes change our Earth. In order to complete the organizer, students must extract and arrange the main ideas from the trade book they've read.

The K-W-H-L strategy, used in a lesson on volcanoes, closely parallels the scientific process of inquiry and engages students in metacognition, or thinking about their own comprehension and learning. Because this lesson requires students to use a variety of resource materials to answer their questions, K-W-H-L also becomes a useful tool for teaching scientific validation.

In the lesson using the discussion web, students practice exploration as they discover facts about life in the Amazon rain forest. In addition, they apply their knowledge of ecosystems in order to answer open-ended discussion questions.

The reading roadmap strategy encourages students to vary their reading speed in order to identify the most important information about the solar system. When students later create their own reading roadmaps, they must decide what concepts are important enough to include.

The expectation outline is another strategy that fosters the scientific process. It requires students to make predictions, ask questions, and explain what prompted their questions prior to reading about Saturn. Students then discover personally relevant information as they read.

The purpose of the anticipation guide is initially to probe students' prior knowledge of weather phenomena and later to refine their understanding. This strategy also requires students to use information from the text to support their responses, a form of scientific validation.

Finally, the knowledge rating and vocabulary self-collection strategies help raise awareness of weather phenomena and how they affect our lives. They are useful because they encourage students to probe their prior knowledge about weather-related terminology and raise questions about unknown terms.

The next section of this chapter explains the strategies in more detail. Each description contains four parts: the first defines the strategy, the second explains the advantages of using it, the third discusses when it is best used, and the fourth lists steps for designing and using the strategy.

Graphic Organizer

What is a graphic organizer?

As described by Richard Barron, the graphic organizer is a pre- or postreading strategy that visually shows relationships among vocabulary or major concepts and supporting details. It can also show how information is organized within a text.

What are the advantages of using a graphic organizer?

The graphic organizer aids comprehension by

— activating prior knowledge,
— relating new information to prior knowledge,

— providing a visual format for organizing information,
— helping students understand relationships among vocabulary and concepts,
— encouraging active participation,
— encouraging higher level thinking.

When is a graphic organizer useful?

A graphic organizer works best with text whose vocabulary or major concepts are interrelated in some way. It works especially well if the students have some prior knowledge of the topic. Graphic organizers may vary greatly in format. For example, a tree diagram shows hierarchical relationships; a pictorial time line shows a causal chain of events; a Venn diagram shows similarities and differences between two concepts. In each case, try to find a form of visual map that shows the relationships you're trying to teach, or one that organizes the information in a way that will aid students' comprehension. The graphic organizer works well in science, but it can be used in other subjects as well.

How do I go about designing and using a graphic organizer?

— Choose the vocabulary or concepts that you want students to learn. Decide how they are related or how the information should be organized so that it is most easily understood.
— Arrange the information into a graphic organizer that illustrates the relationships or organization.
— Include some information in the graphic organizer that the students already know so they can link new knowledge with prior knowledge.
— Share the graphic organizer with the class. If you use it as a prereading strategy, you may share it when it's completely filled in. In that case, describe for the class your arrangement and discuss the entire graphic organizer—that is, use it as an introduction to the material. If, on the other hand, you use the organizer as a postreading strategy, you may leave part of it blank. As before, explain your arrangement to the class. Then ask the students to fill in the missing information. Discuss the entire graphic organizer after everyone has finished.

— Whether you use the graphic organizer as a pre- or postreading activity, a valuable extension activity is to have students design their own graphic organizers for the material learned.
— You may use the graphic organizer in subsequent extension activities, reviews, and tests.

K-W-H-L

What is K-W-H-L?

K-W-H-L is a four-step strategy that encourages students to read text actively. It is an adaptation of Donna Ogle's well-known K-W-L technique. The letters represent the four steps, as follows:

K—What do you *know?*

W—What do you *want* to know?

H—*How* will you find out?

L—What did you *learn?*

The class works together to make a list of what they know about a topic and what they want to know. Then they brainstorm how to find the desired information. (That is the adaptation.) After studying the material, students write what they have learned.

What are the advantages of K-W-H-L?

The K-W-H-L strategy aids comprehension by

— activating prior knowledge,
— having students generate their own questions so they are motivated to read,
— setting a purpose for reading,
— encouraging interaction with the text,
— using a variety of information sources to find answers.

When is K-W-H-L useful?

The K-W-H-L strategy works best when students have some prior knowledge of the topic, because they then have an easier time explaining what they know and what they'd like to learn. Having a variety of sources available rather than relying on a single text helps make the H section more effective and interesting. In addition, K-W-H-L is most valuable when it is used in conjunction with other activities—perhaps experiments, research lessons, or extension activities. It works particularly well in science but can be used in other content areas.

How do I go about using K-W-H-L ?

Make a large display chart that you divide into four sections, one for each letter of the strategy. Write the topic that your class is going to study at the top. Give the students their own personal copies of the chart. For each section, you write the class's ideas; students write their own information on their individual charts.

— For the K section of the chart, students brainstorm what they know about the topic.
— For the W section, the students and you develop a set of questions covering what the class wants to learn.
— For the H section, discuss how the students can find the answers to their questions. Encourage them to consider varied sources of information such as CD-ROMs, encyclopedias, library books, newspaper articles, videos, electronic mail discussion groups or other Internet resources, and experts in the field.
— After the students have finished reading the texts and researching their questions, write what they have learned on the L section of the chart. (You may also want to include a list of questions that the students still want to explore.)

Discussion Web

What is a discussion web?

As Donna Alvermann describes, a discussion web is a post-reading strategy that encourages students to look at both sides of an issue before drawing a conclusion. Students consider a question that asks them to find evidence supporting opposing points of view. They gather their evidence and share it first in small groups and then with the whole class. At the end of the discussion, you may ask students to decide with which point of view they agree.

What are the advantages of a discussion web?

The discussion web aids comprehension by

— encouraging active participation,
— promoting higher level thinking,
— integrating all four of the language arts (oral language and active listening, in particular).

When is a discussion web useful?

A discussion web works best when the text presents an issue with opposing points of view. Both points of view have to be represented by evidence in the text. Students will benefit most if you introduce some kind of extension activity after using the discussion web—for example, writing in a learning log. A discussion web can be adapted for use in all content areas.

How do I go about designing and using a discussion web?

— Write a question that highlights the issue you want the students to consider. Be sure the text includes information explaining the issue from more than one point of view. Also be careful that the question cannot be easily answered. Then divide a page into two columns representing opposing points of view. Place the question in the middle.
— After the students have read the text, give them a copy of the discussion web and ask them to think about the question independently for a short period. Then have

students form pairs to discuss the question using evidence from the text to support both points of view. They write down key words or phrases on the two sides of the web.

— When the students have had a chance to work together for a short time, ask each pair to match up with another pair, so that you have groups of four. The new groups discuss both points of view and students add to their webs as they discuss. Groups should try to reach a consensus on the issue.

— Next, ask the small groups to share their responses with the whole class, explaining their reasoning. Students may want to add information to their own webs.

Reading Roadmap

What is a reading roadmap?

Karen Wood describes the reading roadmap as a guide that shows students how to interact with text. It uses location cues to focus attention on important sections, speed signals to demonstrate that not all text should be read at the same speed, and questions to guide students' reading.

What are the advantages of using a reading roadmap?

The reading roadmap aids comprehension by

— providing a scaffold by showing how readers can interact with difficult text,
— pointing out major concepts and supporting details,
— encouraging students to be selective in their responses to text,
— showing that not all text is equally important,
— encouraging reading at a variety of speeds.

When is a reading roadmap useful?

The reading roadmap works best if students have had prior experience reading at different speeds. In any case, you will need to model using the reading roadmap. In addition, students will need to use roadmaps several times so that they internalize the skill of using different reading speeds. The reading roadmap works well with nonfiction, especially if the text might be too difficult for the students to read without support.

How do I go about designing and using a reading roadmap?

— Decide what major concepts and supporting details you want students to learn from the text. Locate sections in the text that explain those concepts and details.
— Design the reading roadmap, giving students location cues (for example, page numbers), reading speeds (for example, *skim, slow down, read again*), and missions (information to find) for those concepts and details you want them to learn.
— The strategy will most likely work best if you model using the roadmap at first, perhaps doing some sections together as a class.
— After doing a few sections together, ask students to use the roadmap to finish reading the text.
— When the students are finished, use the roadmap as a basis for discussion of the material.
— Students may use the roadmap and information they gather to complete a variety of postreading activities.

Expectation Outline

What is an expectation outline?

The expectation outline is a strategy described by Dixie Lee Spiegal that encourages students to ask questions before reading. After previewing a text, the class discusses what they expect to learn. You write the expectations down in the form of questions, and the students read to find answers.

What are the advantages of using an expectation outline?

The expectation outline increases comprehension by

— raising expectations of what will be read,
— generating student questions about text to be read,
— setting a purpose for reading,
— providing a strategy for gathering information,
— encouraging an active search for meaning.

When is an expectation outline useful?

The expectation outline works well with nonfiction, especially if section headings are used. It is a prereading strategy that works best if students use a postreading activity to answer the questions they've generated.

How do I go about using an expectation outline?

— Ask students to preview the text.
— If the text has section headings, ask the students to name them. Write the section headings on the chalkboard, chart paper, or an overhead transparency, leaving some space underneath each heading.
— Ask the students what they expect to learn from the text. They should state their expectations in the form of questions.
— Write their questions on the expectation outline. Be sure to ask students under which heading to place each question.
— Encourage students to explain what prompted them to ask their questions.
— You may want to add an extra heading, labeled "Other," with no questions listed underneath. This section can be used for extra information that wasn't covered in the questions.
— Students then read the text to find answers to the questions they raised.

Anticipation Guide

What is an anticipation guide?

As described by John Readence and his colleagues, an anticipation guide is a pre- and postreading strategy consisting of a set of statements that reflect a text's major ideas. Students read and react to the statements before reading, with the primary purpose of raising expectations about meaning. After students respond individually, the class discusses their reactions to the statements. Then, the students read to see if the text verifies their reactions. The postreading discussion contrasts the students' initial reactions to the statements with the information presented in the text.

What are the advantages of using an anticipation guide?

The anticipation guide aids comprehension by

— activating prior knowledge,
— setting a purpose for reading,
— encouraging interaction with the text by asking students to formulate a hypothesis and then read to test that hypothesis,
— promoting discussion both before and after reading.

When is an anticipation guide useful?

An anticipation guide works best when students have some prior knowledge of the subject. The statements need to reflect what they have experienced and know. Students benefit even more if they do a follow-up activity in which they write about what they were surprised by and what they learned. This strategy works well in science, but it can be used in other content areas.

How do I go about designing and using an anticipation guide?

— Choose only those major ideas that you want the students to learn, and write a statement about each idea.
— Write the statements so that students are encouraged to use their prior knowledge when thinking about them.
— Individually, students read the statements and mark their reactions (for example, *agree* or *disagree*) on the guide.
— Discuss the students' reactions to the guide before reading.
— Encourage the students to read to find out if the text supports their reactions.
— After the students have read the text, discuss the statements again. Did the text support their prereading reactions?

Knowledge Rating

What is a knowledge rating?

A knowledge rating is a prereading strategy described by Camille Blachowicz that helps students activate what they know about vocabulary. It also allows them to assess how much they know about a topic. Students look at a list of vocabulary and indicate whether they know each word. Afterwards, the class discusses collectively what they know about the vocabulary.

What are the advantages of using a knowledge rating?

The knowledge rating increases comprehension by

— activating prior knowledge,
— encouraging active participation,
— allowing students to share knowledge,
— setting a purpose for reading.

When is a knowledge rating useful?

A knowledge rating works best when students have prior knowledge of some of the vocabulary. Using a knowledge rating before reading will not only assist students, but will allow you to assess how much the students know about a topic. It can be used at the beginning of a unit or with single lessons. A knowledge rating will aid comprehension most if it is used in conjunction with a postreading vocabulary activity. The strategy works well in science, but it can be used in other subjects.

How do I go about designing and using a knowledge rating?

— Use this strategy with text in which vocabulary is essential to comprehension and that contains words about which students may have some prior knowledge.
— Choose the vocabulary you want your students to learn.
— In one column, write the words in list format; then create three additional columns headed "Can Define," "Have Seen/Heard," and "?"

— Ask students to look at the word list before reading the text and mark the column that identifies their level of knowledge of each word.
— Conduct a follow-up discussion revolving around what the students know, think they know, and don't know. Encourage students to share their knowledge of the various words.
— Ask the students to read the text to learn more about the vocabulary listed.
— After studying the text and doing some postreading vocabulary activities, you may go back to the ratings and discuss whether the students would now mark their knowledge of the vocabulary any differently.

Vocabulary Self-Collection Strategy

What is a vocabulary self-collection strategy?

The vocabulary self-collection strategy is a postreading strategy designed by Martha Haggard to aid students in choosing vocabulary to be learned. It also takes advantage of students' interest and prior knowledge to broaden their vocabularies. The students, often in small groups, choose a word they'd like to learn more about or that they think is important to the lesson. Each small group teaches the word to the rest of the class.

What are the advantages of the vocabulary self-collection strategy?

The vocabulary self-collection strategy aids comprehension by

— encouraging active participation,
— allowing students to locate the most important concepts in a piece of text,
— giving practice in using context clues to define vocabulary.

When is a vocabulary self-collection strategy useful?

The vocabulary self-collection strategy works best when vocabulary is essential to learning a text's concepts. Students learn most when the strategy is used several times because they have multiple opportunities to choose the important vocabulary and to use context clues to determine meaning. Your modeling and the students' modeling will illustrate many strategies for choosing important vocabulary and for using context clues.

How do I go about using a vocabulary self-collection strategy?

— After the class has read and discussed a text, students work in small groups to choose a word that they want to learn more about or that they think is important to the lesson. The small group must agree that the word is important for everyone in the class to learn. The group works together to answer the following questions:

> Where is the word found in the text?
> What does the word mean?
> Why should the class learn the word?

— Start by modeling what the students will be doing. Answer the questions about the word you've chosen and give the class time to discuss the definition. They may add more information to the definition based on their knowledge and prior experience. Write the word and its negotiated definition on the board or on a chart.
— Then the small groups teach their words to the class using the same procedure. During each discussion, the whole group and the teacher may add to the definition.
— At the end of the presentations, display all the words and their meanings for the entire class to copy into learning logs or vocabulary lists.
— You may use this student-generated list in subsequent extension activities, reviews, and tests.

THE EARTH'S CRUST

This chapter highlights the topic of the Earth's crust. Curricula designed and used by school districts across the United States and Canada almost always include objectives about how the Earth's crust has developed and how it continues to change. In addition, the American Association for the Advancement of Science, in its 1993 *Benchmarks for Science Literacy*, recommends that information on changes in the Earth's crust be taught by the end of fifth grade, when students are ten or eleven years old.

Lesson 1 uses *Earth Alive!* by Sandra Markle to help students learn about how the Earth's surface changes. Students employ a graphic organizer to explore the many ways that natural events affect our Earth. Lesson 2 uses a variety of resources—many nonfiction trade books, as well as other print and nonprint material—to study volcanoes. Students follow the K-W-H-L strategy to research personal questions on this topic. An annotated list of additional nonfiction trade books about the Earth's crust follows the lessons.

Lesson 1: Exploring Changes to the Earth's Surface

This lesson is for nine- to eleven-year-old students who are studying the Earth's crust. They will read *Earth Alive!* by Sandra Markle (Lothrop, Lee & Shepard, New York, 1991; ISBN 0-688-09361-2, library binding). This engaging book explains how sinkholes, volcanoes, glaciers, weather, and water affect the Earth's crust. It makes excellent use of analogies that are relevant to children, such as comparing oozing magma to toothpaste being squeezed out of a tube. In addition, Markle's writing style encourages students to make predictions while they read.

This lesson could be taught at the beginning of a unit as a way of introducing students to how and why the Earth's crust changes. Or it could be taught near the end of the unit, as a way of summarizing and reviewing. This lesson will most likely take two or three sessions of about 45 minutes each.

OBJECTIVES

Students list and describe natural changes in the Earth's surface. They also observe how information can be organized graphically and discuss the value of using graphic organizers.

I. PREREADING

A. Start a brief discussion about what students saw happening in their neighborhoods that morning. Ask: Does the Earth itself ever move or become active like our neighborhoods do?
B. Briefly discuss the students' responses and list them on chart paper. Save this chart for reference at the end of the lesson.

II. READER-TEXT INTERACTIONS

A. Distribute and introduce *Earth Alive!* by Sandra Markle. Encourage students to look through the text and predict what they think this book may be about. Briefly discuss students' responses.
B. As a class, read page 5 together. Ask: Now what do you think this book will be about?
C. Read pages 6 and 7 to the class as they follow along in their texts. Then ask students to recall the way in which the Earth "became alive." List their responses on the board.
D. Read page 9 to the class. Discuss and list on the board the causes of the sinkhole.

E. Tell students they are going to read a portion of *Earth Alive!* Divide the class into four groups, assigning Group 1 pages 10 to 15, Group 2 pages 24 to 27, Group 3 pages 28 to 32, and Group 4 pages 34 to 38. (You might want to assign pages 10 to 15 and 24 to 27 to average readers, while pages 28 to 32 and 34 to 38 may be more appropriate for less able readers.) Explain to students that as they read, they should look for ways in which the Earth became alive. They should also be aware of why this happened. Encourage students to take notes showing how the Earth became alive. (These notes will help them complete their graphic organizers.)

III. POSTREADING

A. After reading, each group creates a list similar to the sinkhole list: first, they should record how the Earth became alive; next, they should record how and why this happened.
B. Now encourage students to return to the text and look for additional information to add to their lists. Also have them locate and record the page numbers where this information can be found.
C. As a whole group, discuss what each small group has learned and graphically organize the effects of volcanoes, glaciers, wind, and water on the Earth's crust. You may want to create a large graphic organizer on a piece of butcher paper, an overhead transparency, or the board while the students complete smaller versions individually. During your discussion, encourage students to use the information on the lists created in step A to complete the organizer. When appropriate, have students refer back to the text for clarification, validation, or additional information.
D. Briefly review the original question. In what ways does the Earth itself move or become active like our neighborhoods do? Using the information on the graphic organizer, have students describe to a partner two of the ways the Earth naturally changes. (If desired, read page 39 of the text aloud.) Ask the partners to compare their answers to the ones given in the prereading portion of this lesson.

Effects of Volcanoes, Glaciers, Winds, and Water Described in *Earth Alive!*

Volcanoes

p. 11: start deep inside the Earth when solid rock melts
    into magma
p. 11: trapped gases build up pressure
p. 12: magma rises to Earth's surface and forms lava
p. 12: lava forms a volcanic mountain

Glaciers

p. 25: layers of snow pile up in mountain valleys
p. 25: move because they weigh a lot
p. 25: move slowly or fast
p. 26: center of glacier moves faster than rest of glacier
p. 26: pick up rocks as they move
p. 27: make rivers and lakes when they melt

Winds

p. 29: can move large boulders
p. 29: lift sand and carry it away
p. 31: form sand dunes
p. 31: can blow away topsoil
p. 32: can create black blizzards

Water

p. 34: can wash away or erode the shoreline
p. 34: can erode a hillside
p. 34: can erode a cliff
p. 34: rivers can carry rocks away
p. 35: rivers can form canyons like the Grand Canyon
p. 37: rivers can dump fine soil, or sediment, on land

Earth Alive! Graphic Organizer

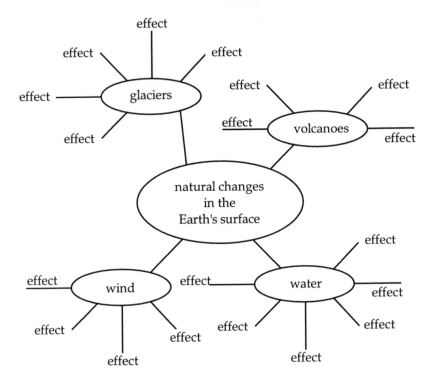

E. Discuss the value of using graphic organizers. Ask: How might this graphic organizer help you?

F. On the following day, cover the graphic organizer and have students write in their learning logs or science journals what they learned about how and why natural changes in the Earth's surface occur. Have students share their responses.

IV. OPTIONAL ACTIVITIES

A. Have students look in the media for information on natural changes in the Earth's surface—for example, volcanoes, hurricanes, floods, earthquakes, and tornadoes.

B. Incorporate experiments that deal with the concept of erosion from Janice VanCleave's *Earth Science for Every Kid* (see p. 34 for a full description of this book). Examples of experiments that would make appropriate follow-ups to this lesson are numbers 42, 44, 46, 47, 52, and 112.

Lesson 2: Learning about Volcanoes

This lesson is designed for nine- to eleven-year-old students who are studying Earth science. The goals of the lesson are to demonstrate that we gain information from a variety of sources, and to show that it is important to validate that information since different sources don't always agree. This lesson would be appropriate at the beginning, in the middle, or at the end of a unit on the Earth's crust. It will take approximately six sessions of 45 minutes each.

OBJECTIVES

Using K-W-H-L, students engage in scientific inquiry and scientific validation of self-selected topics related to volcanoes.

RECOMMENDED BOOKS AND MATERIALS

Following is a list of nonfiction trade books that are appropriate for this lesson. In addition to trade books, have other print and nonprint research materials available. These may include CD-ROMs, encyclopedias, newspaper articles about volcanoes, videos, travel brochures, rock samples, copies of seismographic charts, and addresses for electronic mail discussion groups interested in or web sites focused on Earth science. Check with your regional math and science centers or science museums for help in locating e-mail addresses and other materials.

Franklyn Branley's *Volcanoes* (HarperCollins, New York, 1985; ISBN 0-690-04431-3, library binding, 0-06-445059-7, paperback) is part of the Let's Read and Find Out science series. Its straightforward text offers brief overviews of famous volcanoes and their disastrous effects, plate tectonics, how volcanoes are created, and why they erupt. While it does not go into great depth, its smooth style and creative drawings make it enjoyable reading.

Volcano! by Maurice Krafft (Young Discovery Library, Ossining, NY, 1993; ISBN 0-944589-41-3, library binding) offers concise one-or two-page sections highlighting many aspects of volcanoes. These include how volcanoes are formed, the life cycle of a volcano, their destructive and beneficial impact on the environment, and what it means to be a volcanologist. Well done pictures and diagrams accent the text.

In addition to describing the causes, locations, and types of volcanoes found around the world, Christopher Lampton's *Volcano* (Millbrook Press, Brookfield, CT, 1991; ISBN 1-56294-028-7, library binding, 0-395-63645-0, paperback) makes reference to historic volcanoes, the benefits of volcanic eruption, and methods used to predict volcanic activity. Each chapter includes two to three pages of text, complemented by photos, maps, and diagrams. The book is part of the A Disaster! Book series, which includes titles on blizzards, earthquakes, forest fires, hurricanes, and tornadoes.

Volcano: The Eruption and Healing of Mt. St. Helens by Patricia Lauber (Bradbury Press, New York, 1986; ISBN 0-689-71679-6, paperback) provides a delightful description of Mt. St. Helens in the state of Washington, USA, and clearly illustrates the life cycle of a volcano. Photos taken before and after the eruption show stark contrasts and often include people or machinery to illustrate scale. The chapter on colonizers and survivors discusses the interdependence of species and would work well in a unit on ecosystems.

Seymour Simon introduces *Volcanoes* (Morrow, New York, 1988; ISBN 0-688-07412-X, library binding) in an interesting manner by discussing both the mythological and modern-day explanations of how volcanoes form. The four groups of volcanoes—shield, cinder cone, strato, and dome—are then described by photos that depict their distinguishing characteristics. Analogies are used to explain concepts such as plates and movement. Some users may find the lack of page numbers inconvenient.

Janice VanCleave's *Earth Science for Every Kid: 101 Easy Experiments that Really Work* (John Wiley & Sons, New York, 1991; ISBN 0-471-54389-6, library binding, 0-471-53010-7, paperback) includes fairly simple and effective experiments that don't require a science lab. It covers a wide range of concepts in seven categories: Earth in Space, Rocks and Minerals, Crustal Movement, Erosion, Atmosphere, Weather, and

Oceans. The purpose statements included with the experiments make it easy to match them with topics being covered in the classroom.

The innovative format of *Eyewitness Science: Earth* by Susanna Van Rose (Dorling Kindersley, New York, 1994; ISBN 1-56458-476-3, library binding) introduces many Earth science subjects such as water and ice, oceans, rocks, continental drift, and volcanoes. Each section offers a brief overview of the topic, then adds capsules of information on related items. The text is accompanied by eye-catching pictures which command the reader's attention. It would be best used as a classroom library book, as would its companions in the Eyewitness Science series.

I. PREREADING

A. Show students photographs of volcanoes. Tell them they are going to be studying volcanoes for the next few days. Show them the books and materials you have assembled and ask why you might have assembled such a variety. (This leads into the objectives of the lesson.)

B. Before you suggest that students look at the materials, discuss with them what they already know about volcanoes. Divide a large sheet of chart paper into four sections. Label one section "What We Know about Volcanoes." Record students' responses. This section forms the K component of the K-W-H-L chart.

C. Ask students to think about what they would like to learn about volcanoes. Demonstrate by writing a question you may have in the second section of the chart, "What We Want to Know about Volcanoes." Examples might include: How can volcanoes be predicted? How did our ancestors explain volcanoes? Encourage students to use *what, when, where, who, why,* and *how* when forming questions. Record students' questions in the second section, under your own. This section makes up the W component of the K-W-H-L chart.

D. Have pairs of students select one question from the list or create one original question about volcanoes. To carry out the scientific validation component of the lesson, encourage at least two pairs of students to select similar research questions. Students should write their question in their learning logs.

E. Before students use the materials you have collected, discuss with them how scientists conduct their research. Lead students to realize that scientists learn by "doing"—for example, by experimenting or observing—and by "using" other resources such as fellow scientists, books, videos, computers, and magazines. Tell the students they are going to act as scientists when they answer their own questions.

F. Label the third, or H, section of the K-W-H-L chart "How We Can Learn More about Volcanoes." Ask students for ways that scientists answer their own questions and record the responses in this column.

II. READER-TEXT INTERACTIONS

A. Give the students time to examine the materials you've assembled. Encourage them to record in their learning logs the sources that might help them answer their personal research questions.

B. Briefly discuss how to locate information using an index, a table of contents, or other text features. Also discuss and demonstrate how scanning helps us find information, while skimming allows us to read that information quickly to determine whether it will be useful. (If need be, these techniques could become the focal points of mini-lessons.)

C. To avoid student plagiarism and to encourage active reading during the research process, have students locate appropriate materials and examine them for 10 to 15 minutes, then put the materials out of sight and write in their learning logs a summary of what they just learned. To begin the validation process, have students return to their materials and confirm what they have recorded in their logs. If misinformation was included, have students correct themselves by deleting it and adding the accurate information. In addition, have students record bibliographical details such as title, author, and page number.

D. Continue C until students have located appropriate information from a variety of sources.

III. POSTREADING

A. Begin a discussion of the process of scientific validation. Remind students they have already begun the validation process by "using" other resources and by reading, taking notes from memory, and going back to the original source to check the accuracy of their notes.

B. Explain another step in the validation process, which involves communication among scientists who share the findings of their research. Remind students that they are acting as scientists. Team up pairs that have similar research questions so that they may discuss their findings. Encourage your scientists to verify the accuracy of the information they have gathered by returning to the materials they have used.

C. To emphasize the "doing" aspect of scientific validation, explain that scientists also learn by conducting experiments and observing. To do this, they use the scientific process. Review the scientific process (formulating a question, creating a hypothesis or prediction, collecting data through observation, analyzing the data to confirm or reject the hypothesis, attempting to answer the original question). Demonstrate the process by doing experiment 22 from Janice VanCleave's *Earth Science for Every Kid*. Use the following procedure:

1. Describe the phenomenon and display the materials to be used.
2. Present the question to be investigated.
3. Formulate a hypothesis or prediction.
4. Follow the procedure for the experiment.
5. Observe what happens.
6. Speculate why this happened and compare with hypothesis/prediction.
7. Attempt to answer the original question posed in #2 above.
8. Validate your results by reading the explanation VanCleave provides.
9. Formulate new questions for future experiments.

Now introduce the "My Investigation Report" form and have students complete it for experiment 22.

A sample Report Form Completed for Experiment 22 from *Earth Science for Every Kid*

MY INVESTIGATION REPORT

Scientist's name ALLISON _____ Date 5/15 _____

The **question** to be investigated: What will happen to the cardboard circle when we put our hands that we've rubbed together around the bottle?

What we **predicted**: the cardboard circle will fly off.

The **materials** my group used: lightweight cardboard (oaktag), glass bottle, scissors, refigerator, cup of water.

The **procedure** used: 1) Cut a circle from oaktag that is slightly larger than the top of the bottle. 2) Place empty bottle in the freezer for 20 minutes. 3) Remove the bottle from the freezer 4) Dip the cardboard into the cup of water and place it over the mouth of the bottle. 5) Quickly rub the palms of your hands together about 20 times. 6) Immediately place your hands around the bottle.

What we **observed**: One side of the cardboard circle rises and falls.

MY INVESTIGATION REPORT (page 2)

A drawing
of our
experiment

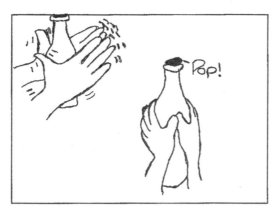

Pop!

Look at your **original question**. What happened? The cardboard popped up when the bottle was rubbed by our hands.

Why do we **think** this happened? The heat from our hands made the air inside the bottle expand and the expanded air pushed up on the cardboard and made it pop.

Other **variables** we could change are: size of hands, number of times rubbed, type of bottle, number of minutes in the freezer

Choose one variable and write a **new question** to investigate. What will happen to the cardboard circle when we put bigger hands around the bottle? What will happen if hands are rubbed only 10 times?

D. Have students self-select one of experiments 23, 30, 37, or 38 from the VanCleave text. Students who select the same experiment will work cooperatively as a team of scientists. Meet with each group and describe the phenomenon with which they are experimenting. Help each group formulate a question to be investigated as well as a hypothesis. Give each scientist a blank "My Investigation Report" form as well as a list of materials and procedures for the experiment selected. Have teams carry out their experiments and record their results.

E. Have each group report its results to the whole class and record them on a class results chart.

F. As a closure activity, complete the fourth column of the K-W-H-L chart by recording "What We Have Learned." Encourage students to list not only what they have learned about volcanoes, but also what they have learned about scientific inquiry and scientific validation.

G. An additional closure activity is to have the students write about what they have learned about volcanoes in their science journals or learning logs the following day.

IV. OPTIONAL ACTIVITY

A. As a culminating activity, have students build a chemical volcano using potting soil or sand, baking soda, and vinegar.

Additional Books about the Earth's Crust

Branley, Franklyn. *Earthquakes*. New York: HarperCollins, 1990. ISBN 0-690-04663-4, library binding; 0-06-445135-6, paperback.

This colorful, easy-to-read yet informative book discusses why earthquakes happen, what their devastating effects can be, where the Earth's danger zones are, and what measures people can take to safeguard themselves from earthquakes. Drawings, maps, and diagrams complement the text.

Clark, John. *Earthquakes to Volcanoes: Projects with Geography*. New York: Glouster Press, 1992. ISBN 0-531-17316-X, library binding.

Clark, John. *Earthquakes to Volcanoes: Projects with Geography*. New York: Glouster Press, 1992. ISBN 0-531-17316-X, library binding.

Each two-page spread forms a "chapter" that focuses on a single concept related to the Earth. These concepts include earthquakes, volcanoes, rock formation, folds and faults, formation of oceans, erosion, and unusual landscapes. Each chapter contains an introduction, an explanation of the concept, illustrations, and photographs. Some chapters include a "Did You Know?" section or a "How to Build a Model" section. Very high visual appeal.

Horenstein, Sidney. *Rocks Tell Stories*. Brookfield, CT: Millbrook Press, 1993. ISBN 1-56294-238-7, library binding.

This well-written, carefully organized book uses photographs and text to describe the value of rocks, how they change over time, and what rocks reveal about the Earth and its history. This book not only provides ample information about rocks, but it could be used in a lesson on parts of a book or using an index and glossary.

Lauber, Patricia. *Seeing Earth from Space*. New York: Orchard Books, 1990. ISBN 0-531-08502-3, library binding.

Beautiful photographs of volcanic islands, salt lakes, mountains, rivers, fault lines, and crops, which illustrate how small and fragile the Earth truly is, form the core of this visually stunning book. In addition, a complex description of remote sensing and how scientists use it to study weather, plant life, and man's influence on our changing planet is given. This text could also be used in a unit on ecosystems.

Simon, Seymour. *Earthquakes*. New York: Morrow, 1991. ISBN 0-688-09634-4, library binding.

This book is a good introduction to earthquakes. It describes how faults move, what faults look like on the Earth's surface, what types of instruments are used to measure earthquakes, and the damage caused by them. The full-color photos and illustrations dramatically depict the information in the text. Some users may find the lack of page numbers inconvenient.

Simon, Seymour. *Icebergs and Glaciers*. New York: Morrow, 1987. ISBN 0-688-06187-7, library binding.

Packed with information, this book describes where glaciers originate, what they're made of, how and why they move, how fast they move, and the visible effects of moving glaciers. It also describes the formation of icebergs, the size of icebergs in relation to American states and other countries, and uses of icebergs. Most points of reference are within the United States. Some users may find the lack of page numbers inconvenient.

THE ENVIRONMENT AND ECOLOGY

The topic of the environment and ecology is of great concern to many people, as evidenced by its emphasis in science curricula developed in the United States and Canada over the past ten years. *Benchmarks for Science Literacy* recommends that information on the environment be taught by the end of fifth grade.

All of the lessons in this chapter use *Antonio's Rain Forest* by Anna Lewington (Carolrhoda, Minneapolis, MN, 1993; ISBN 0-87614-749-X, library binding). This story of how people live in the Amazon rain forest is narrated by one of its eight-year-old inhabitants. It highlights his surroundings, his daily life, and his father's work as a rubber tapper. Also included are short informational sections which describe how rubber is made and used. The vivid photographs and delightful writing make the rain forest come to life for young readers.

Each lesson is about a separate section of the text. Lesson 1 uses chapter 1 to introduce rain forests and the people who live in them. Students use a Venn diagram, a type of graphic organizer, to help them compare and contrast their own lives with Antonio's life. Lessons 2 and 3 use chapters 2 to 4 to emphasize the importance of the rain forest's plants and animals and their interrelationships. Different kinds of graphic organizers help the students keep track of the vast array of life that flourishes in this environment. Lesson 4 uses chapter 5 to describe how the people of the rain forest have negotiated with the Brazilian government concerning the forest's use. Students use a discussion web to help them see both sides' views. A fifth and optional lesson (to be used after students have finished reading the book) describes a hands-on activity that helps students understand what happens to plant and animal life when sections of the rain forest are destroyed. An annotated list of additional nonfiction trade books about the environment and ecology follows the lessons.

Lesson 1: Introducing the Rain Forest

Chapter 1 is entitled "Antonio's Home" and describes Antonio's family; where they live; where they get their food, medicine, and clothing; and how Antonio's father earns his living. This lesson serves as an introduction to rain forests and the people who live in them. It will take approximately 45 minutes to complete.

OBJECTIVE

Students use a Venn diagram to compare their lives with Antonio's life.

I. PREREADING

A. Before introducing *Antonio's Rain Forest*, ask students to respond to the following questions in their learning logs or science journals: What do you know about the rain forest? What specific things would you like to learn about the rain forest? Share and discuss the responses.

B. Tell students they are going to begin reading *Antonio's Rain Forest* by Anna Lewington. Mention that the book is about Antonio, a young Brazilian boy. Suggest that because Antonio has never traveled away from his home in the rain forest, he has no idea what their lives may be like. Ask: If you could tell Antonio something about yourself, what would it be? Encourage students to describe their families, what they like to do in their spare time, what kind of houses or apartments they live in, and where they get their food, clothing, and medicine. List student responses on the board.

A Venn Diagram for Chapter 1 of *Antonio's Rain Forest*

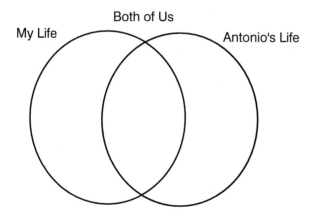

Both of Us

My Life   Antonio's Life

C. Distribute a Venn diagram to each student. Ask students to list information about themselves that they would like to share with Antonio in the "My Life" section of the Venn diagram.

II. READER-TEXT INTERACTIONS

A. Distribute and introduce the book by drawing students' attention to the table of contents, the many color photographs, the glossary, and the index.
B. As a class, look at page 6 and make predictions about what this chapter might contain. Remind students that since Antonio lives in Brazil, he speaks Portuguese. Encourage students to look for the Portuguese words in the chapter. Also encourage them to set a personalized purpose for reading such as "I'd like to find out what Antonio does with his spare time."
C. Read pages 6 through 13 aloud, or have students read silently.

III. POSTREADING

A. After reading, discuss Antonio's life in the rain forest. During the discussion, have students fill in the "Antonio's

Life" section of the Venn diagram. Encourage students to use the Portuguese terms whenever possible.

B. Using the information from both sides of the Venn diagram, discuss how Antonio's life is similar to yet different from the students' lives. Lead them to realize how we all depend, to some extent, on the rain forest for our survival.

C. Have students complete the middle section of the Venn diagram by listing the ways that Antonio's life is similar to theirs.

D. Using the information on the Venn diagram, have students write a letter to Antonio telling him what life is like in their community. If possible, try to arrange actual pen pals for your students by contacting the agencies listed on page 47 of *Antonio's Rain Forest*.

E. Revisit this chapter and, as a whole group, skim and scan it for Portuguese words. Write these words and their definitions on chart paper. Continue to add to this chart as new Portuguese words are encountered in subsequent lessons. If desired, incorporate some of these words into students' weekly spelling or vocabulary tests.

Lesson 2: *Plants and Animals of the Rain Forest*

Chapter 2 is entitled "Along the Forest Trail." It describes plants and animals found in the rain forest and how Antonio's family interacts with them. The lesson will take approximately 45 minutes to complete.

OBJECTIVE

Students explain the significance of plants and animals found in the rain forest using a graphic organizer to keep track of the information presented in the text.

I. PREREADING

A. Remind students of their Venn diagram comparing Antonio's life with their own. Point out that plants and animals are very important to people who live in the rain forest. Ask: In what ways do *we* depend on plants and animals for our survival?

A Graphic Organizer for Chapter 2 of *Antonio's Rain Forest*

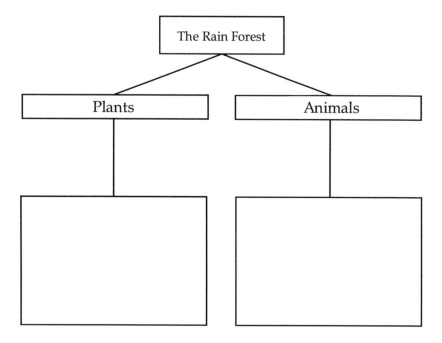

II. READER-TEXT INTERACTIONS

A. Tell students that chapter 2 describes some of the plants and animals that share the rain forest with Antonio. As they read the chapter, they should use a graphic organizer to list the kinds of plants and animals Antonio encounters along the forest trail.

III. POSTREADING

A. Discuss some of the plants and animals that students read about in this chapter. For example, you might ask: Are all of these animals friendly? Which ones does Antonio avoid? Why does he avoid them? If people who live in the rain forest get sick or hurt, what do they do? Guide students to discover the interdependence of living things in the rain forest by reminding them of how we depend on plants and animals for our survival.
B. Encourage students to become experts by researching one type of plant or animal found in the rain forest. They

can use encyclopedias, books, CD-ROMs, films, television documentaries, and other sources of information. Suggest to students that they focus on locating information that explains how humans use or benefit from the plants and animals found in the rain forest. If students choose an animal to research, they could also incorporate information regarding its classification, diet, habitat, and general characteristics, as well as its place in the food chain, into their reports. They could write about their findings on a piece of colored paper cut in the shape of the animal or plant they have selected. Decorate your bulletin board with their creations.

Lesson 3: All about Rubber

Chapter 3 is entitled "Tapping Rubber" and explains how Antonio's father taps rubber trees in order to extract rubber latex. Chapter 4, "Making Rubber," explains the process Antonio's father and the other *seringueiros* use to turn the latex into rubber. Chapter 4 also explains the relationship between the *seringueiros* and the *patroes*, or rubber barons, and the *seringueiros'* struggle to gain economic freedom.

OBJECTIVE

Students explain the interdependence and interrelationships of living things in an ecosystem.

METHOD

You may choose how you wish to approach these chapters. For instance, *prior to reading,* you may want to introduce the concept of interdependence by explaining the food chain. Perhaps you'll choose to read these chapters aloud to your students, or students might take turns reading to a partner.

After reading you might point out the important role the *seringueiros* play in *our* everyday lives. Show students pages 24 and 28 of the text, which outline some of the ways in which we use rubber. Have students brainstorm additional ways rubber is used in modern society—for example, in the soles of our sneakers, around our car windows, and around the doors of our refrigerators. Also remind students of the plants and animals they researched as a chapter 2 activity. Reiterate how humans benefit from the rain forest's plants and animals in order to reinforce the concept of interdependence within an ecosystem. One idea is to make a two-column chart as a class. In one column, list plants, animals, and products of the rain forest. In the second column, list their modern-day uses.

Lesson 4: Exploring Point of View

Chapter 5 is entitled "A New Life in the Forest" and describes how the *seringueiros* worked with the Brazilian government to develop a plan to protect their corner of the rain forest while maintaining their lifestyle. This lesson will take approximately two sessions of 45 minutes each to complete.

OBJECTIVE

Students use a discussion web to broaden their perspectives on the effects humans have on the environment and ecosystems.

I. PREREADING

A. Start a discussion about point of view by offering various points of view concerning the rain forest. For example, many people who do not live in the Amazon region are concerned about its deforestation because of the environmental effects and because of our dependence on the plants, animals, and products made from raw materials found in the rain forest. However, ask students also to consider how a Brazilian cattle rancher, who sells his beef to McDonalds, might feel if he needed more room for his cattle and wanted to cut down rubber trees growing on his property. Or discuss the Brazilian citrus grower who wants to plant more orange trees so he can sell his juice oranges to Tropicana. How would his actions affect citrus growers in Florida or Spain? The goal is to have students consider various points of view about an issue.

Discussion Webs for Chapter 5 of *Antonio's Rain Forest*

Discussion Web 1

Antonio's family   da Silva and others

What does each of these people
get from the rain forest?

How does each of them use
the rain forest?

Discussion Web 2

Antonio's family   da Silva and others

How has the rain forest
changed as a result of the
way people used it?

Discussion Web 3

Antonio's family   da Silva and others

How can Antonio's family and
da Silva use the rain forest
without destroying it?

II. READER-TEXT INTERACTIONS

A. Introduce chapter 5 by telling students it presents some different points of view about the rain forest. Discuss what points of view might be presented. Ask students to look for these points of view as they read.

III. POSTREADING

A. As you distribute blank discussion web forms to the students, remind them of your prereading discussion about point of view.
B. Pose the following questions about Antonio and the other *seringueiros* and da Silva and the other *patroes*: What does each of these people get from the rain forest? How does each of them use the rain forest? Write the questions in the center of the discussion web you have drawn on the board or chart paper. Ask students to write them on their individual copies.
C. Have students independently think of possible responses to each question for a few minutes.
D. With a partner, students take turns jotting down responses to the questions. Encourage students to maintain an equal number of responses in each column—that is, for every response written under the Antonio and the *seringueiros* heading, a response should be written for da Silva and the *patroes*.
E. Now, form quads of students by having two sets of partners work together. Their task is to share the responses they have each generated in step C regarding Antonio's and da Silva's points of view about the rain forest.
F. As a whole group, discuss how Antonio's family depends on the rain forest for survival and how da Silva depends on the rain forest for economic development. Throughout your discussion, encourage students to add information to their discussion webs.
G. Repeat steps C, D, E, and F using discussion web 2. This web addresses the question "How has the rain forest changed as a result of the way these people used it?"
H. Conclude your lesson by having students complete a third discussion web focusing on how the rain forest can be used without endangering it. Then ask students to

write a paragraph or two on this topic. Give students time to share their written responses with their classmates.

Lesson 5: The Effects of Deforestation

This optional lesson would make a good culminating activity to your study of *Antonio's Rain Forest*.

OBJECTIVE

Students engage in a hands-on activity to see what happens to the species within a rain forest when sections of it are destroyed. Students grasp the concept of extinction and explain the effects of deforestation.

MATERIALS

— *Antonio's Rain Forest*
— small bags of color-coated chocolates
— survival spreadsheet grids
— overhead transparency and projector (optional)

METHOD

A. Pose the following question to students: What do you think happens to the different species of animals when areas of the rain forest are destroyed? List the responses and predictions on the board.
B. Distribute the survival spreadsheet grids, books, and candies to each student.
C. Have the students choose species of animals that will be represented by each color of candy and write the species name beside each color on the grid. For example, the red candies could represent the pica pau bird, and the blue candies could represent tucandera ants. For reference, encourage the students to use their chapter 2 graphic organizers.
D. When the students have assigned a species to each color, explain to them that the blocks on their survival spread sheet grids represent sections of the rain forest.
E. Have the students pour the contents of their bags of candy onto the grids so that the chocolates are scattered all over. (You may choose to do this on an overhead.)

Survival Spreadsheet Grid for Culminating Activity
for *Antonio's Rain Forest*

Red: _____
No. before _____
No. after _____

Yellow: _____
No. before _____
No. after _____

Blue: _____
No. before _____
No. after _____

Orange: _____
No. before _____
No. after _____

Green: _____
No. before _____
No. after _____

Brown: _____
No. before _____
No. after _____

F. Have students count the number of each species (that is, of each color of candy) and record the numbers next to their particular species at the bottom of the grid. Have students share their recordings.

G. "Destroy" one section of the rain forest at a time (block by block) by removing all of the species in a given section. As the sections are destroyed, students may eat the candies.

H. Repeat G until three-quarters of the rain forest has been destroyed.

I. Now have each student record the number of each particular species remaining on the grid.

J. Have students compare their new species counts with their old ones, and then share their counts and discuss their responses.

K. Ask for student comments regarding the significance of this activity as it relates to extinction. Guide students to the realization that when even a small section of the rain forest is destroyed, an entire species can become extinct.

L. Ask students to respond to this activity by writing in their journals or learning logs. Encourage them to write about the effects of deforestation on animal species.

Additional Books about the Environment and Ecology

Baines, John. *Protecting the Oceans.* New York: Steck-Vaughn, 1991. ISBN 0-8114-2391-3, library binding; 0-8114-3454-0, paperback.

This book is a colorful and interesting description of the importance of the world's oceans and many of the problems facing them and their inhabitants. It gets the reader actively involved in debating the solutions to these problems by detailing opposing points of view.

Brown, Mary Barrett. *Wings along the Waterway.* New York: Orchard, 1992. ISBN 0-531-08581-3, library binding.

The superb watercolors of a variety of water fowl included in this delightful book are sure to capture both the reader's heart and attention. Descriptions of these endangered birds include information about their food sources, shelter, and habitats, and obstacles to their survival. Each story-like section focuses on a particular type of bird. This would be a wonderful addition to any classroom where ecological issues are being studied.

Cherry, Lynne. *A River Ran Wild.* San Diego, CA: Harcourt Brace, 1992. ISBN 0-15-200542-0, library binding.

This book chronicles the environmental history of the Nashua River in New England (Massachusetts and New Hampshire, USA) from its discovery by Native Americans through its becoming polluted beginning in the industrial revolution and finally to the ambitious clean-up that revitalized it. Beautiful watercolors and colored pencil drawings illustrate this history. There is something for everyone in this book.

Cone, Molly. *Come Back, Salmon.* San Francisco, CA: Sierra Club, 1992. ISBN 0-87156-572-2, library binding.

The students at Jackson School cleaned Pigeon Creek, restocked it with salmon, and preserved it as an unpolluted place for salmon to spawn. Readers of all ages will be excited by the monumental achievements made in this small town in the state of Washington, USA. A beautifully told and inspirational story.

Foster, Joanna. *Cartons, Cans, Orange Peels: Where Does Your Garbage Go?* New York: Clarion, 1991. ISBN 0-395-56436-0, library binding; 0-395-66504-3, paperback.

This book lives up to its title by giving an in-depth answer to the question it poses. It follows garbage from curbside to destinations such as dumps, landfills, compost piles, and recycling plants, explaining the operation and environmental consequences of each. Kids will enjoy this practical discussion of garbage.

Lampton, Christopher. *Oil Spill.* Brookfield, CT: Millbrook Press, 1992. ISBN 1-56294-071-6, library binding. Part of the A Disaster! Book series.

Extremely accurate and full of facts about oil and oil spills, this book provides a solid survey of a man-made disaster. It describes not only some of the worst oil spills of all time but also gives detailed background information on what oil is, and why it is so important to us. The book's deficiency in the area of interesting illustrations may be due to the subject matter.

Love, Ann & Jane Drake. *Take Action: An Environmental Handbook for Kids*. New York: Tambourine, 1993. ISBN 0-688-12465-8, paperback.

This coherent, well-written text is packed with relevant illustrations and motivational activities. Content focuses on the importance of preserving nature, threats to plant and animal species, and what kids can do to protect the environment. It would make a wonderful classroom resource or birthday gift.

McVey, Vicki. *The Sierra Club Kid's Guide to Planet Care and Repair*. San Francisco, CA: Sierra Club, 1993. ISBN 0-87156-567-6, library binding.

Each chapter uses excellent examples, analogies, and anecdotes that are relevant to children to illustrate important concepts. Exercises for the imagination, concrete methods to prevent further environmental damage, the importance of recycling, and a focus on refusing to buy over-packaged goods are unique features of this text. Refreshing and wonderfully written!

Pearce, Fred. *The Big Green Book*. New York: Grosset & Dunlap, 1991. ISBN 0-448-40142-8, library binding.

This book explains why Earth is a comfortable place to live and the dangers facing the planet, and argues that we all must work together to keep it safe and healthy for future generations. The illustrations are superb because they visually clarify complex concepts in a manner easy for children to understand.

Pringle, Laurence. *Oil Spills: Damage, Recovery, and Prevention*. New York: Morrow, 1993. ISBN 0-688-09861-4, library binding.

This information-packed book explains what petroleum is, what it is used for, and the many ways in which both large and small amounts are spilled. The text concludes by explaining how oil spills can be averted. Good information, but not much visual appeal.

Temple, Lannis. *Dear World: How Children Around the World Feel about Our Environment*. New York: Random House, 1993. ISBN 0-679-84403-1, paperback.

Children from 40 nations contributed to this wonderfully inspiring book. Both the original and translated texts provide and promote discussion of the differences in languages, while photos of the children show us how remarkably similar people from around the world are in many ways. Very motivational for kids.

Wilkes, Angela. *My First Green Book: A Life Size Guide to Caring for the Environment*. New York: Knopf, 1991. ISBN 0-679-91780-2, library binding.

This colorful, motivating text features activities for children that simulate acid rain, show the effects of water pollution, and demonstrate how recycling and planting a wildlife garden help our environment. A book that will require children to use their minds as well as their hands.

. . . .

SPACE

American and Canadian science curricula developed in the past ten years consistently list learning about space as an objective for nine- to eleven-year-old students, and in the United States it is recommended that information on space be taught by the end of fifth grade. In addition, elementary students are often fascinated with space and are motivated to learn about it.

Lesson 1 in this chapter uses *Our Solar System* by Ian Graham to teach basic information about the solar system. Students use and design their own reading roadmaps to help them negotiate the text. Lesson 2 uses Gregory L. Vogt's *Saturn* to teach about that planet. An expectation outline helps students set purposes for their reading and provides a means for gathering information. An annotated list of additional nonfiction trade books about space follows the lessons.

Lesson 1: A Tour of the Solar System

In this lesson, students read *Our Solar System* by Ian Graham (Two-Can, London, 1991; distributed in the U.S. by Scholastic; ISBN 0-590-47622-X, paperback). It contains factual descriptions of the planets, our moon, and the sun, and a brief section on comets, meteors, and asteroids. Sections are devoted to a single body or a group of bodies and include capsulized facts and colorful pictures. A description of how to build a model space probe and a story simulating what space travel may be like in 2050 are added to the end of the book.

The lesson would probably work best as an introduction to a unit on the solar system. Students may want to do more thorough research on some aspect of the solar system after studying this book. This lesson will most likely take six sessions of about 45 minutes each.

OBJECTIVES

Students use reading roadmaps to learn about the solar system and the different objects that make it up. After the strategy has been modeled and the class has used a reading roadmap together, students design a map for a section of text. In addition, pairs of students develop a way of demonstrating knowledge learned from *Our Solar System* and share it with the class.

I. PREREADING

AIntroduce the topic of the solar system by using the quiz located on page 29 of the book. Read the statements aloud and ask the students to mark on paper whether they think they are true or false. Briefly discuss the students' answers, always asking them for their reasoning. Introduce *Our Solar System* to the class by telling them that it is the source of all the answers to the quiz, and lots more information as well. Point out that the quiz is located in the back of the book.

II. READER-TEXT INTERACTIONS

A. Distribute *Our Solar System* and reading roadmap 1 (covering pages 4 to 9) to the students. Follow the roadmap for pages 4 and 5 as a large group. First, discuss with the students how the map's mission statements and questions help them focus their attention on particular aspects of the text. As the group reads, model the suggested reading speed for the students, and continue to model the different speeds throughout the lesson. Discuss the strategy of reading quickly or scanning the text for particular facts. Now draw the students' attention in particular to the different reading speeds posted for subsequent pages. Point out that just as streets have speed limits that vary, so too the reading roadmap includes different reading speeds.

B. Continue as a large group to use the reading roadmap to read and discuss pages 6 to 9 of *Our Solar System*. In addition to discussing the material, ask the students to explain how the map helped them read, understand, and remember the information. Discuss how the speed signs helped them vary their reading speeds for different parts of the text. Discuss why it is important to read with varying speeds.

C. Divide students into heterogeneous groups and distribute reading roadmap 2, for pages 10 and 11 and a review of pages 4 to 11. Introduce the three new reading speeds on the map and discuss them. Remind students that they will once again be varying their reading speeds and review why this is important.

D. Have students read pages 10 and 11 and reread pages 4 to 11 while using their roadmaps. Encourage them to discuss the text and the map as they read and work together. Discuss the roadmaps as a whole group.

E. Explain to the students that they are going to design reading roadmaps for the rest of the book and distribute master maps to them. As a large group, brainstorm different speeds that students might use and different "missions" they might try. Read page 12 together and decide what speed and mission to put on the master roadmap for that page. Then, divide the class into four groups. Students in two of the groups will read pages 13 to 17 and use the first part of the master to design their map for those pages. The other two groups will use the second part to design their map for pages 18 to 22. (You may choose to give the students two sessions to complete this activity.)

F. Once the groups have finished reading their sections and designing their roadmaps, have them trade and use a student-generated roadmap to read the section they haven't studied yet.

Reading Roadmap for Our Solar System

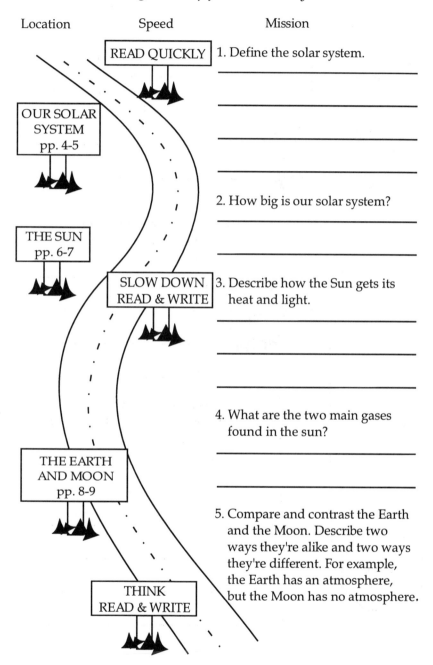

Location   Speed   Mission

READ QUICKLY   1. Define the solar system.

OUR SOLAR
SYSTEM
pp. 4-5

THE SUN
pp. 6-7   2. How big is our solar system?

SLOW DOWN   3. Describe how the Sun gets its
READ & WRITE   heat and light.

                  4. What are the two main gases
                     found in the sun?

THE EARTH
AND MOON
pp. 8-9   5. Compare and contrast the Earth
                     and the Moon. Describe two
                     ways they're alike and two ways
                     they're different. For example,
THINK   the Earth has an atmosphere,
READ & WRITE   but the Moon has no atmosphere.

Reading Roadmap for Our Solar System

Location   Speed   Mission

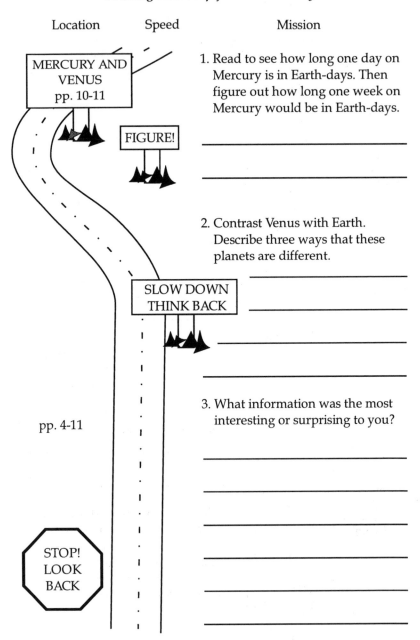

MERCURY AND VENUS pp. 10-11

FIGURE!

SLOW DOWN THINK BACK

pp. 4-11

STOP! LOOK BACK

1. Read to see how long one day on Mercury is in Earth-days. Then figure out how long one week on Mercury would be in Earth-days.

_____

_____

2. Contrast Venus with Earth. Describe three ways that these planets are different.

_____

_____

_____

_____

3. What information was the most interesting or surprising to you?

_____

_____

_____

_____

_____

Master Reading Roadmap for Pages 12-22 of Our Solar System

Location	Speed	Mission
Mars, p. 12		_____
		_____
		_____

Part I

Roadmap Designers: _____

Mars, p. 13

_____

_____

Jupiter,
pp. 14-15

_____

_____

Saturn,
pp. 16-17

_____

_____

pp. 12-17

_____

_____

_____

Part II

Roadmap Designers: _____
Uranus, Neptune,
and Pluto,   _____
pp. 18-19
                          _____

                          _____

Comets, Asteroids,   _____
and Meteorites,
pp. 20-21   _____
Space Probes, p. 22
pp. 18-22   _____

                          _____

A. After all the students have finished, use the roadmaps to discuss pages 13 to 22. Be sure to take time to discuss what different groups found important enough to include on the maps. Discuss again how the roadmaps with their speed signs helped students when reading the text. Take time to talk about how the students might use the road-maps to help them in the future.

B. Look again at the quiz on page 29. Read the statements a second time and ask the students to compare their two sets of answers. Discuss changes in the students' answers and reasoning.

C. Ask the students to work with their partners to develop a way to demonstrate their learning from *Our Solar System*. Remind them to refer to their reading roadmaps for help. For example, students might design a way to remember the nine planets and the asteroid belt in the correct order. They could develop a mnemonic, a song or rap, a visual of some kind, a dance movement, a number sequence, or a game. Allow time for all pairs to showcase their method for the rest of the class.

IV. OPTIONAL ACTIVITIES

A. Read *Postcards from the Planets* by David Drew (Black Cockatoo Publishing, Wentworth Falls, Australia, 1988; ISBN 0-7312-1011-5, paperback). In this book, a collection of postcards from Jessie and Kate to their grandpa, written during their trip on a futuristic space bus, conveys interesting and relevant information about our solar system. The planets, the sun, and the moon are each covered in a one-page section which consists of a postcard and a picture. What it lacks in depth of information, the book makes up for in high interest level and springboard potential. After reading, students can use the facts they learned to create and write postcards from the planet of their choice to family members. They could describe climate, temperature, and surface features of their planet.

B. Have students choose a planet. Place them in groups according to their choice. Each group makes a papier-mâché planet that can be hung from the ceiling to create a classroom solar system.

Lesson 2: Focus on Saturn

In this lesson, students read *Saturn* by Gregory L. Vogt (Millbrook Press, Brookfield, CT, 1993; ISBN 1-56294-332-4, library binding; part of the Gateway Solar System series). Scientists' attempts to view Saturn—from Galileo's first glimpses to the Hubble Space Telescope's keen eye—introduce this book. It goes on to give a detailed description of the planet, including a discussion of its rings and moons, based primarily on information gained from the U.S. space probes Pioneer 11, Voyager 1, and Voyager 2, and from the Hubble telescope. Colorful pictures make the book visually appealing.

The lesson might best fit in a unit on the solar system. After the students have been introduced to all the planets, this book could be used to study Saturn in particular. The lesson is designed to be adapted for use with any book on a particular planet or group of planets. Students could also use the expectation outline described in this lesson independently or in small groups whose members share the same interests. The lesson will most likely take four sessions of about 45 minutes each.

OBJECTIVES

Students describe, compare, and explain the features of Saturn and its moons. They also use an expectation outline to set purposes for reading and as a strategy for gathering information.

I. PREREADING

A. Distribute *Saturn* to the students. Give them time to explore the book. Ask them to find the section headings, and then list them on the board, chart paper, or a transparency, leaving space underneath each one. (The headings are Spacecraft Study Saturn, The Sixth Planet, The Rings, and Saturn's Moons.)
B. Ask: Based on these headings, what information about Saturn do you expect to find in this book? Have students state their expectations in the form of questions. For example, a student might ask, "How many moons does Saturn have?" Make an expectation outline by writing the students' questions under the appropriate section head-

ings. Be sure to ask students under which headings they think the questions should go and to explain what prompted them to ask their questions. They may want to refer to their previewing of the text.

C. Make a copy of the expectation outline for each student. Include an extra heading, "Other," with no questions under it. Students may use this category as a place to make note of other interesting or important information they encounter as they read.

II. READER-TEXT INTERACTIONS

A. Distribute the expectation outline to the students and ask them to read *Saturn*. (You may choose to have the students read alone or in pairs.) As they read, they should look for answers to the questions they asked on the expectation outline. The students can write brief notes answering the questions, along with the page number where they found the information. Encourage them to write down under the "Other" heading any details that aren't related to the questions. They may also want to jot down new questions that come to mind while reading.

III. POSTREADING

A. Ask the students to work in small groups to write detailed answers to the questions for one of the book's sections.

B. The information that each group gains can be shared with the class in a variety of ways. First, the group can decide on how to share what they've learned—perhaps a panel discussion, a set of posters, a filmstrip, or a written report to be read to the class. In addition, each member of the group could meet with members from all the other groups and teach them the material (a jigsaw approach borrowed from cooperative learning). Whatever way the students share their learning, the rest of the class can make detailed notes on what they've learned on their own expectation outlines.

C. As a whole group, discuss what the students learned about Saturn, what they found most interesting, and what they're still curious about. (Perhaps some of the students' questions won't have been answered, or new questions may have arisen. Then you could have a brief discussion about how to find those answers.) Also, discuss how the expectation outline helped the students read *Saturn*, and how they could use an expectation outline with other books.

D. On a half sheet of paper or an index card, ask students to write an anonymous "exit slip" that summarizes what they learned or found most interesting as they studied Vogt's book. Then collect them. Exit slips are a way of bringing closure to what was learned, as well as to help establish direction for the next lesson. For instance, you may choose to read them aloud the following day as a way to review the material, or you may decide to pursue further study of topics students have identified as interesting.

Additional Books about Space

Asimov, Isaac. *How Did We Find Out about Neptune?* New York: Walker, 1990. ISBN 0-8027-6982-9, library binding.

The book is clearly written, with explicit cohesion and organization. The first three chapters pique the reader's interest by sounding more like a mystery than a science book. However, it is not visually interesting—the print is small and the illustrations are black-and-white drawings.

Couper, Heather & Nigel Henbest. *How the Universe Works: 100 Ways Parents and Kids Can Share the Secrets of the Universe.* Pleasantville, NY: Reader's Digest, 1994. ISBN 0-89577-576-X, library binding.

There are six chapters in this detailed study of the universe: Spaceship Earth, The Moon, The Solar System, The Sun, The Stars, and The Cosmos. Each chapter begins with a two-page introduction that is fairly difficult reading yet provides good background information. Activities and experiments complete each chapter; the experiments are clearly and simply explained using step-by-step photos, and the materials they require are easily found in the home. This book is an excellent resource.

Estalella, Robert. *Our Star: The Sun.* Hauppauge, NY: Barron's Educational Series, 1993. ISBN 0-8120-6370-8, library binding.

This title in the Window on the Universe series includes a wealth of information on the sun. Topics include the sun's structure, its effects on Earth, and its unique features. Each topic is covered in a two-page section, with one page devoted to text and the other to illustrations that graphically show what the text describes. This book would be best used with fairly advanced readers who have already been studying the sun.

Estalella, Robert. *The Stars*. Hauppauge, NY: Barron's Educational Series, 1993. ISBN 0-8120-6371-6, library binding; 0-8120-1738-2, paperback.

This fact-filled book, also part of the Window on the Universe series, details stars from their birth to their death, explaining difficult subjects such as why they shine, black holes, pulsars, and supernovas. It accents these discussions with diagrams that relate well to the text. Like the other books in this series, it would be best used with fairly advanced readers who already have some knowledge of the topic.

Gallant, Roy A. *101 Questions and Answers about the Universe*. New York: Macmillan, 1984. ISBN 0-02-736750-9, library binding.

A question-and-answer format is used to cover a vast range of topics that would interest both children and adults. Most areas of the solar system are touched on, including the planets, the sun, and the moon; also included are discussions of the stars and theories of the universe's formation. Though it lacks color pictures, this delightfully written reference book, packed with lots of informative tables, would be an excellent addition to a classroom library.

Harris, Alan & Paul Weissman. *The Great Voyager Adventure: A Guide through the Solar System*. Englewood Cliffs, NJ: Messner, 1990. ISBN 0-671-72538-6, library binding.

Superbly documented with photos, this well-written summary carefully describes the planning involved in the Voyager missions, including an explanation of how many problems were solved. The text also includes detailed information and photographs of Jupiter, Saturn, Uranus, and Neptune. Sure to delight the space buffs in your classroom.

Lauber, Patricia. *Journey to the Planets*. New York: Crown, 1990. ISBN 0-517-54477-6, library binding; 0-517-59029-8, trade hardcover binding.

This book contains separate chapters on the planets (Uranus, Neptune, and Pluto are covered together), the moon, and the origin of our solar system. Each section details not only what we know, but what we would like to know about the topic. The chapter on Earth gives much information about our atmosphere and the crust's movements. A good reference book for the classroom or school library.

Lauber, Patricia. *Meteors and Meteorites: Voyagers from Space*. New York: Crowell, 1989. ISBN 0-690-04632-4, library binding.

Lauber's clear and concise writing style helps to keep the reader's interest as she describes asteroids, comets, dinosaurs, and meteorites. This would also be a good reference book for the classroom or school library.

Reddy, Francis. *Rand McNally's Children's Atlas of the Universe*. Chicago, IL: Rand McNally, 1990. ISBN 0-528-83408-8, library binding.

This book offers detailed coverage of the major and minor celestial bodies in our solar system, the stars, our galaxy, and the universe. The guide to the night sky at the end of the book will delight the young stargazers in your class. It would be best used as a student-and-teacher reference book.

Ride, Sally & Tam O'Shaughnessy. *The Third Planet: Exploring the Earth from Space*. New York: Crown, 1994. ISBN 0-517-59362-9, library binding.

Breathtaking photos of Earth taken from space shuttles are used to describe our planet. These illustrations are exceptionally clear and colorful. The accompanying explanations are thoughtfully written and the organization is easy to follow. A great book!

Ride, Sally & Tam O'Shaughnessy. *Voyager: An Adventure to the Edge of the Solar System*. New York: Crown, 1992. ISBN 0-517-58158-2, library binding.

After describing the Voyager missions, this book takes the reader on a ride along their paths. You encounter Jupiter,

Saturn, Uranus, and Neptune in all their splendor, with close-up pictures taken from the two spacecraft. The text provides information on each planet, highlighting the discoveries made by the Voyagers.

Ridpath, Ian. *The Facts on File Atlas of Stars and Planets*. New York: Infobase Holdings, 1993. ISBN 0-8160-2926-1, library binding.

Well planned and organized, this book concisely covers the sun, moon, planets, and stars. The text is aided by wonderful pictures and detailed captions. It fails only in the star chart section, which is difficult to understand. Although this is a reference book, sections could be used to teach lessons about a particular subject.

Simon, Seymour. *Space Words: A Dictionary*. New York: HarperCollins, 1991. ISBN 0-06-022533-5, library binding.

Seventy-nine space-related words are defined in this dictionary. There are never more than two or three definitions on a page, and every other page has only one definition. Almost all words have colorful illustrations. When difficult words are used, easier synonyms are provided in parentheses (for example, *revolve* is clarified by *circle*). Cross-references are also used (for example, a student looking up *falling star* is directed to *See meteor*). No pronunciations are provided.

Stott, Carole. *I Wonder Why Stars Twinkle and Other Questions about Space*. New York: Kingfisher, 1993. ISBN 1-85697-881-8, library binding.

The question-and-answer format allows the reader to quickly gain lots of basic information about space. The style is clear and easy to read. Some of the examples are funny (for example, Io, one of Jupiter's moons, is described as looking like a cheese-and-tomato pizza) and the illustrations clarify the text well. It would be an excellent book to use at the beginning of a unit on planets.

The Visual Dictionary of the Universe. New York: Dorling Kindersley, 1993. ISBN 1-56458-336-8, library binding.

This book is not a typical dictionary. It contains only one broad term for every two pages, hence the definitions are long and detailed with lots of well-labeled illustrations included for clarification. As a result, the book includes a huge amount of information. The organization is not alphabetical—rather it goes from large concepts (universe) to smaller concepts (asteroids). Charts are included in the back that give astronomical data about planets, the sun, comets, moons, eclipses, galaxies, and stars.

Vogt, Gregory. *Jupiter*. Brookfield, CT: Millbrook Press, 1993. ISBN 1-56294-329-4, library binding. Part of the Gateway Solar System series.

Basic facts such as Jupiter's great size, gravity, gaseous composition, and information on the Great Red Spot are detailed in the first section of this book. The second part focuses on recent exploration of Jupiter and its moons and the possibility of new discoveries and mysteries from the Galileo mission. The glossary and For Further Reading sections included in all the books in this series are useful and concise.

Vogt, Gregory. *Neptune*. Brookfield, CT: Millbrook Press, 1993. ISBN 1-56294-331-6, library binding. Part of the Gateway Solar System series.

This book details the search for Neptune, the mysterious planet nobody could see. It also includes information on the planet and its moons. In addition, surprises concerning Neptune's great spot and rings discovered by Voyager 2 are included. Explanations of difficult concepts are clear and easy to understand.

Vogt, Gregory. *Uranus*. Brookfield, CT: Millbrook Press. ISBN 1-56294-330-8, library binding. Part of the Gateway Solar System series.

Like the other books in the series, *Uranus* gives the most up-to-date information based on Voyager 2's observations. This book describes the spacecraft's findings about Uranus's rings, satellites, atmosphere, and unusual tilt. The Quick Facts section allows for easy comparisons to the other planets covered in the series.

. . . .

WEATHER

Science curricula developed over the past ten years often include the study of weather, and in the United States it is recommended that this topic be taught by the end of fifth grade. The two books we chose to use in this chapter do an exceptionally fine job of explaining why we have the weather we do. In Lesson 1, students use an anticipation guide to help them interact with *Storms* by Seymour Simon as it describes how thunderstorms, tornadoes, and hurricanes develop. Lesson 2 uses Hiscock's *The Big Storm* to teach about how and why storms develop and how they change as they move across the Earth.

Students use a knowledge rating, the vocabulary self-collection strategy, and a pictorial time line to help them describe the atmosphere, weather conditions, and seasonal changes in weather. An annotated list of additional nonfiction trade books about weather follows the lessons.

Lesson 1: Studying Storms

In this lesson, students read *Storms* by Seymour Simon (Morrow, New York, 1989; ISBN 0-590-46320-9, paperback). In this book, Simon describes thunderstorms, tornadoes, and hurricanes. He discusses how they form, what happens as they occur, and why they die out. He also explains how to protect oneself from these storms. The dramatic photos do a good job of clarifying the text. The lesson could fit in more than one place in a weather unit. It could be used as an introduction to storms, in which case it might motivate students to do more research on one of the book's topics after the lesson. Or it could be used near the end of the unit as a way to check and verify previous learning. The anticipation guide includes statements for all of the major topics covered in the book, though you may choose to use only those statements that fit your curricular needs. (Note that *Storms* does not have page numbers. You may want to number the pages before beginning the lesson.) The lesson will most likely take three sessions of about 45 minutes each.

OBJECTIVES

Students describe weather conditions during thunderstorms, tornadoes, and hurricanes. They use an anticipation guide to activate prior knowledge and set purposes for reading. They locate information the author provides as evidence to support main ideas.

I. PREREADING

A. Start a discussion about storms. Ask: What do you know or think about storms?
B. Distribute the anticipation guide and explain that it has some statements about storms. Ask the students to read the guide and, in the Before Reading column, to put a plus sign by those statements with which they agree and a minus sign by those with which they disagree. If students are unsure, suggest they make an educated guess.
C. When the students are finished with the guide, discuss their responses, encouraging them to explain the reasons for their beliefs. Accept valid reasoning.

II. READER-TEXT INTERACTIONS

A. Divide the class into two groups and ask students to find a partner in their group. Distribute a copy of *Storms* to each pair of students. Assign pages 1 to 17 and statements 1 to 10 to the pairs in one group and pages 18 to 28 and statements 11 to 19 to the remaining pairs.
B. Ask the pairs to read their assigned sections together to see if their beliefs about the statements on the anticipation guide were correct. If the text changes their minds

about any statements, they should re-mark with a plus or minus in the After Reading column. Encourage the pairs to discuss the text as they read it together.

III. POSTREADING

A. As a whole group, discuss the reading by going back over the statements and examining which of the students' beliefs were correct and incorrect. Ask the students to refer to the text to verify their responses. (All students should listen carefully to see what the students in the other group discovered from the text.)
B. Take some time to talk about the anticipation guide. How did it help students? Why did it help?
C. So that all students are familiar with the material, ask the pairs to read the pages they did not study in the Reader-Text Interactions phase.
D. Discuss surprises and facts the students learned.
E. Remind students that part of the anticipation guide activity was to use the text to verify information. Tell students that in informational text, it is important that the author provide evidence to support the points made. Now write the following statement from page 1 on the board, on chart paper, or on a transparency: "Thunderstorms are the most powerful electrical storms in the atmosphere." Ask: What evidence does Seymour Simon provide to prove this statement? Have students refer to the text to look for evidence. List their responses under the statement.
F. Have the students go back to their original partners. Give each pair one (or more) statement(s) from *Storms*, such as "Hailstorms sometimes cause great damage" (page 9), "Lightning can be very dangerous" (page 16), "Tornadoes sometimes do strange things" (page 22), or "Hurricanes are the deadliest storms on Earth" (page 24). Their task is to locate and record the information Simon provides as evidence for these statements. Have students prove each statement with three facts.
G. Discuss the evidence students located in F. Ask: Why is it important for authors to provide evidence when writing an informational book? What should we do when we write our own informational books?

Anticipation Guide for *Storms* by Seymour Simon

Name_____ Date _____

Directions: Before reading *Storms*, take a moment to read each of the following statements. Use the Before Reading column to put a + next to each statement with which you agree and a - next to each statement with which you disagree. Be prepared to support your decision. If any of your beliefs change after reading, put a + or - in the After Reading column.

Before Reading	After Reading	
_____	_____	1. In 20 minutes, a single thunderstorm can drop 125 million gallons of water.
_____	_____	2. Thunderstorms form when moist air near the Earth's surface is heated by the sun.
_____	_____	3. A thunderstorm cloud may grow to be one mile wide and 4,000 feet high.
_____	_____	4. Thunderstorms are part of the Earth's air-conditioning system.
_____	_____	5. Hail may be as big as a grapefruit.
		6. Windshears can be dangerous to aircraft.
_____	_____	7. The temperature of a single bolt of lightning can reach 75,000°F.
_____	_____	8. Lightning can only spark from the clouds to the ground.
_____	_____	9. You can usually hear thunder from six or seven miles away.
_____	_____	10. Light is about a million times faster than sound.
_____	_____	11. If you are outside during a thunderstorm, protect yourself by lying down on the wet ground.
_____	_____	12. Some tornadoes travel at more than 100 miles per hour.
_____	_____	13. A tornado's winds can whirl around the funnel at speeds of 200 miles an hour or more.
_____	_____	14. The safest place during a tornado is in the cellar.

     _____   _____ 15. Tornadoes sometimes can pick up cars or trains and put them back down without damaging them.

     _____   _____ 16. Hurricane winds blow at least 74 miles per hour and sometimes more than 200 miles per hour.

     _____   _____ 17. If you are in the eye of a hurricane, the winds blow the hardest and the sky is black.

     _____   _____ 18. *Hurricane* and *typhoon* are different names for the same kind of storm.

     _____   _____ 19. Scientists have learned all that they can about thunderstorms.

H. As an additional measure of what the students learned about storms, have them respond in their learning logs or science journals to the question "What did you learn about storms?"

IV. OPTIONAL ACTIVITY

A. Have students collect and report on newspaper articles on the various storms mentioned: thunderstorms, hail storms, tornadoes, hurricanes, and typhoons.

Lesson 2: Tracking a Storm

In this lesson, students will read *The Big Storm* by Bruce Hiscock (Atheneum, New York, 1993; ISBN 0-689-31770-0, library binding), which tells the story of a huge storm that swept across the United States in the spring of 1982. *The Big Storm* is written in a narrative style, but it explains weather phenomena (wind, fronts, air pressure, thunder, lightning) in a clear and simple manner. The book is beautifully illustrated with many full-page watercolors.

The lesson would probably work best as an introduction to a unit on weather. It will most likely take three sessions of about 45 minutes each.

Knowledge Rating for *The Big Storm* Vocabulary

How much do you know about these weather words? Put an X in the column that best describes your level of knowledge of each word.

Word	Can Define	Have Seen/ Heard	?
westerlies	_____	_____	_____
cold front	_____	_____	_____
low pressure center	_____	_____	_____
Severe Weather Watch	_____	_____	_____
thunder	_____	_____	_____
snow	_____	_____	_____
avalanches	_____	_____	_____
atmosphere	_____	_____	_____
barometric pressure	_____	_____	_____
tornado	_____	_____	_____
lightning	_____	_____	_____
hail	_____	_____	_____
front	_____	_____	_____
barometer	_____	_____	_____
jet stream	_____	_____	_____
updraft	_____	_____	_____
rain	_____	_____	_____

OBJECTIVES

The students describe the atmosphere, weather conditions, and some seasonal changes in weather. They use a knowledge rating to activate prior knowledge about weather. In addition, they teach self-selected vocabulary from the text to the rest of the class. Finally, students create a pictorial time line of *The Big Storm* by placing vocabulary words in the appropriate locations.

I. PREREADING

A. Do a knowledge rating with the students using vocabulary words from *The Big Storm*. Use the students' ratings as a starting place for a discussion on what they know about weather. Encourage students' explanations of words and discussion of where they learned about them.
B. Explain that the book they are about to read uses the vocabulary from the knowledge rating in its description of a particular storm that crossed the United States in April 1982.

II. READER-TEXT INTERACTIONS

A. Distribute *The Big Storm* to the students. You may have them read individually, or you may choose to let them read in pairs.
B. Ask the students to read to find out what happened during this "big storm" and also to learn about the vocabulary of which they were unsure. Encourage them to make note of the places in the text that explain the words. If the students are in pairs, remind them to discuss the text as they read it together.

III. POSTREADING

A. After the students have finished the reading, introduce the vocabulary self-collection strategy. Ask small groups of students to nominate words they would like to teach to the rest of the class. (Most likely they'll choose words from the knowledge rating, but they may also choose others.) The teams should answer the following questions for each of their chosen words: Where is the word found in the text? Based on the context or other references, what do you think the word means? Why did your team think the class should learn the word? Each team should then choose a spokesperson to present the words to the class by reporting the team's answers to these questions. This strategy will work best if you model it first—that is, if you present a nominated word and answer the above questions. During the student presentations, you can assist by encouraging discussion, writing the words and their definitions on the board or a chart, and inviting other class members to add information about the words' meanings. You may ask students to copy the negotiated meanings into a learning log.

B. Ask the students to look at the pictorial time line near the front of *The Big Storm*. Discuss why the words are placed where they are. For example, why is *snow* placed on March 31 on the time line? Ask each team to decide where its words would best fit on the time line. As a large group, draw your own time line for *The Big Storm* (on the board or mural paper) and write the vocabulary words where the teams and class agree they belong.

C. Return to the knowledge rating. Ask the students to fill it out again using a different colored pen, now that they've read *The Big Storm* and studied the vocabulary. Discuss whether the students' knowledge of the words' definitions has changed after reading the text. (Students most likely will have a fuller understanding of words they thought they knew, such as *rain*, *snow*, or *thunder*.) Take some time to talk about how the knowledge rating, vocabulary self-collection strategy, and time line helped students learn the vocabulary and thus learn about basic weather phenomena. Why did they help?

IV. OPTIONAL ACTIVITY

A. Have each student present a vocabulary word to the class by means of a skit, poster, experiment, book, cartoon, or drawing. You may wish to videotape the presentations.

Additional Books about Weather

Allen, David. *Air: All about Cyclones, Rainbows, Clouds, Ozones and More.* Toronto: Greey de Pencier, 1993. ISBN 1-895688-08-6, paperback.

Delightfully illustrated, this text does a superb job of defining and visually clarifying all sorts of things about air: its chemical components, instruments used in measuring it, wind and wind storms, types of clouds, weather prediction, the atmosphere, effects of air pollution, and how you can care for the air.

Branley, Franklyn. *Hurricane Watch*. New York: Harper Trophy, 1985. ISBN 0-690-04471-2, library binding; 0-06-445062-7, paperback.

This title in the Let's Read and Find Out series explains how hurricanes form, what paths they take, the destruction they cause, and how weather-watchers track them. Clearly written and beautifully illustrated, this is an excellent text for students just starting their study of hurricanes.

DeWitt, Linda. *What Will the Weather Be?* New York: HarperCollins, 1991. ISBN 0-06-021597-6, library binding.

This book provides a simple, easy-to-understand explanation of weather concepts. Fronts and air pressure are explained, as are the tools meteorologists use to help predict the weather. It would be a good book to use to introduce weather after a K-W-L activity, especially with low readers.

Kahl, Jonathan. *Weatherwise: Learning about the Weather*. Minneapolis, MN: Lerner, 1992. ISBN 0-8225-2525-9, library binding.

This book is a great introductory text for the young meteorologist. Many weather subjects such as the atmosphere and water cycle, weather patterns, precipitation, and forecasting are briefly explained with colorful illustrations and diagrams. It would make a useful classroom resource book.

Kahl, Jonathan. *Wet Weather: Rain Showers and Snowfall*. Minneapolis, MN: Lerner, 1992. ISBN 0-8225-2526-7, library binding.

All facets of wet weather are discussed, including the water cycle, clouds and their formation, fronts, air masses, precipitation, and severe weather. Crisp photographs and clear diagrams added to difficult passages bring the concepts to life. This factual, interesting approach will delight nine- to eleven-year-olds.

Lampton, Christopher. *Blizzard*. Brookfield, CT: Millbrook Press, 1991. ISBN 1-56294-029-5, library binding; 0-395-63641-8, paperback. Part of the A Disaster! Book series.

A good reference tool for classes studying storms and winter weather, this book includes sections on why it snows, what a blizzard is, famous blizzards of the past, and what to do in case of a blizzard. It does have a tendency to focus on the United States and Canada, so it may not lend itself to a study of global weather.

Lampton, Christopher. *Drought!* Brookfield, CT: Millbrook Press, 1992. ISBN 1-878841-91-2, paperback. Part of the A Disaster! Book series.

This book provides a rich source of information for students who are studying weather disasters. It focuses on the nature of past droughts and makes predictions about future ones. Although the majority of photos are of places within the United States, the text does address worldwide droughts with a few accompanying photos. The chapter on prehistoric droughts adopts the theory of evolution, and in some chapters the conceptual load is heavy (for example, hydrolic cycle and causes of drought) for the low to average reader.

Lampton, Christopher. *Tornado.* Brookfield, CT: Millbrook Press, 1991. ISBN 1-56294-032-5, library binding; 0-395-63644-2, paperback. Part of the A Disaster! Book series.

Like the others in the series, this book will become an often-used reference in your classroom. Students who are fascinated by tornadoes will get to read about and see what happens when the power of a tornado is unleashed, how tornadoes are formed, and, most important, what to do when one is spotted. This book focuses solely on the United States.

Lee, Sally. *Hurricanes.* New York: Franklin Watts, 1993. ISBN 0-531-20152-X, library binding; 0-531-20152-X, paperback.

Good organization makes this book a very usable resource for students wanting more information on hurricanes. Graphic photos and clear diagrams aid the text in describing how hurricanes form, what their structure is, what happens when they make landfall, and how meteorologists forecast and track them. The last section on science projects gives useful ideas for related activities.

Leslie, Clare Walker. *Nature All Year Long.* New York: Greenwillow, 1991. ISBN 0-688-09183-0, library binding.

This book provides a description of how each month's weather affects nature. Four-page sections for each month have one full-page illustration and three pages of text with lots of smaller illustrations. There are many activities throughout the book, and a "facts box" within each section provides interesting details about each month. The region described is the northeastern United States, but the information is general enough that students in any area could use it as a starting point for studying nature throughout the year. This book would act as a good bridge between weather and ecology units.

McVey, Vicki. *The Sierra Club Book of Weather Wisdom*. Boston, MA: Little, Brown, 1991. ISBN 0-316-56341-2, library binding.
   This book is filled with information on how to become "weatherwise." Each chapter builds on the last, making text cohesion excellent. End-of-chapter activities are included. Many chapters have narratives (marked by special borders) that tell stories of weatherwise children from around the world. The activities and stories would be appropriate for all students; the exposition is best for average to advanced readers.

. . . .

PROFESSIONAL

BIBLIOGRAPHY

Alvermann, D. "The Discussion Web: A Graphic Aid for Learning across the Curriculum." In *The Reading Teacher*. Vol. 45, No. 2 (1991).

Armbruster, B.B. & T.H. Anderson. *Content Area Textbooks* (Reading Education Rep. No. 23). Urbana, IL: University of Illinois, Center for the Study of Reading, 1981.

American Association for the Advancement of Science. *Benchmarks for Science Literacy*. New York: Author, 1993.

Barron, R. "The Use of Vocabulary as an Advance Organizer." In *Research in Reading in the Content Areas: First Report*. H.L. Herber & P.L. Sanders (Eds.). Syracuse, NY: Syracuse University Reading and Language Arts Center, 1969.

Blachowicz, C. "Making Connections: Alternatives to the Vocabulary Notebook." In *Journal of Reading*. Vol. 29, No. 7 (1986).

Burke, E.M. & S.M. Glazer. *Using Nonfiction in the Classroom*. New York: Scholastic, 1994.

Haggard, M.R. "The Vocabulary Self-Collection Strategy: Using Student Interest and World Knowledge to Enhance Vocabulary Growth." In *Journal of Reading*. Vol. 29, No. 7 (1986).

Irwin, J.W. & C.A. Davis. "Assessing Readability: The Checklist Approach." In *Journal of Reading*. Vol. 24, No. 2 (1980).

Ogle, D.M. "KWL in Action: Secondary Teachers Find Applications that Work." In *Reading in the Content Areas: Improving*

Classroom Instruction (3rd ed.). E.K. Dishner, T.W. Bean, J.E. Readence, & D.W. Moore (Eds.). Dubuque, IA: Kendall-Hunt, 1992.

Readence, J.E., T.W. Bean, & R.S. Baldwin. *Content Area Reading: An Integrated Approach.* Dubuque, IA: Kendall-Hunt, 1981.

Richards, P. O. "Thirteen Steps to Becoming a Children's Literature Expert." In *The Reading Teacher.* Vol. 48, No. 1 (1994).

Spiegal, D.L. "Six Alternatives to the Directed Reading Activity." In *The Reading Teacher.* Vol. 34, No. 8 (1981).

Sudol, P. & C.M. King. "Teaching Reading: A Checklist for Choosing Nonfiction Trade Books." In *The Reading Teacher.* Vol. 49, No. 5 (1996).

Vacca, R.T. & J.L. Vacca. *Content Area Reading* (4th ed.). New York: HarperCollins, 1993.

Wood, K.D. "A Guide to Subject Matter Material." In *Middle School Journal.* Vol. 19, No. 1 (1988).

THE PIPPIN TEACHER'S LIBRARY

The titles in this series are designed to provide a forum for interpreting, in clear, straightforward language, current issues and trends affecting education. Teachers are invited to share—in their own voice—the insights, wisdom and knowledge they have developed out of their professional experiences.

Submissions for publication are welcomed. Manuscripts and proposals will be reviewed by members of the Pippin Teacher's Library Editorial Advisory Board, chaired by Lee Gunderson, PhD, of the University of British Columbia.

Members of the editorial Advisory Board are:
Karen Feathers, PhD, of Wayne State University.
Richard McCallum PhD, of the University of California, Berkeley.
Jon Shapiro, PhD, of the University of British Columbia.
Jan Turbill, MEd, of the University of Wollongong, New South Wales.
David Wray, PhD, of the University of Exeter, England.

Written submission should be directed to:
The Editorial Director
Pippin Publishing Corporation
85 Ellesmere Road
Suite 232
Toronto, Ontario
Canada
M1R 4B9

INFOTEXT : READING AND LEARNING
Karen M. Feathers

*Classroom-tested techniques for helping students overcome
the reading problems presented by informational texts.*

WRITING IN THE MIDDLE YEARS
Marion Crowhurst

*Suggestions for organizing a writing workshop approach
in the classroom.*

AND THEN THERE WERE TWO:
CHILDREN AND SECOND LANGUAGE LEARNING
Terry Piper

*Insights into the language-learning process help
teachers understand how ESL children become bilingual.*

IN ROLE: TEACHING AND LEARNING DRAMATICALLY
Patrick Verriour

*A leading drama educator demonstrates how easily drama can be used
to integrate learning across the curriculum.*

LINKING MATHEMATICS AND LANGUAGE: PRACTICAL
CLASSROOM ACTIVITIES
Richard McCallum, Robert Whitlow

*Practical, holistic ideas for linking language—both reading
and writing—and mathematics.*

TEACHING THE WORLD'S CHILDREN
Mary Ashworth, H. Patricia Wakefield

*How early childhood educators and primary teachers can help
non-English-speaking youngsters use—and learn—English.*

THE MONDAY MORNING GUIDE TO COMPREHENSION
Lee Gunderson

*Strategies for encouraging students to interact with,
rather than react to, the information they read.*

LOOK AT ME WHEN I TALK TO YOU:
ESL LEARNERS IN NON-ESL CLASSROOMS
Sylvia Helmer, Catherine Eddy

*How culture influences the messages we give—and receive—
and how this affects classroom practice.*

PARTNERSHIPS IN LEARNING:
TEACHING ESL TO ADULTS
Julia Robinson, Mary Selman

Practical ideas for forming rewarding partnerships with adult ESL learners.

SO . . . YOU WANT TO TEACH ADULTS?
Elizabeth Williams

An adult educator explores collaborative philosophies and techniques that work with adult learners.

AN ENGLISH TEACHER'S SURVIVAL GUIDE:
REACHING AND TEACHING ADOLESCENTS
Judy S. Richardson

The story of an education professor who returns to a high-school classroom determined to put theory into practice.

LANGUAGE, LITERACY AND CHILDREN WITH SPECIAL NEEDS
Sally M. Rogow

Successful approaches to welcome and help integrate children with special needs into mainstream classrooms— so that good learning happens for everyone!

LEARNING TOGETHER IN THE MULTICULTURAL CLASSROOM
Elizabeth Coelho

A valuable compendium of practical ideas for making group work function successfully in a multicultural context.

USING STUDENT-CENTERED METHODS WITH TEACHER-CENTERED ESL STUDENTS
Marilyn Lewis

Practical and affirmative advice for teachers welcoming teacher-centered students to their classes: how to help them, how to let them enjoy success.

LIFEWRITING: LEARNING THROUGH PERSONAL NARRATIVE
Sydney Butler, Roy Bentley

How students can become real writers by telling the stories of their lives.

LITERACY ACTIVITIES FOR BUILDING CLASSROOM COMMUNITIES
Ardith Davis Cole

*A wealth of creative activities that will help your
students enjoy their learning even more!*

THOUGHTFUL TEACHERS, THOUGHTFUL LEARNERS: A GUIDE TO
HELPING ADOLESCENTS THINK CRITICALLY
Norman J. Unrau

*Practical strategies for helping guide adolescents to
think reflectively with minds open to examining critical
issues from a wide variety of perspectives.*

KEYS TO LITERACY FOR PUPIL AT RISK
Lee Dobson, Marietta Hurst

*Finding the strengths that even the most reluctant pupil
possesses and using them to make learning successful.*